SO
FAR

SO FAR

words from learners

Edited by JEAN BENNETT, RICHARD JACCOMA *and* LEE WEINSTEIN

Photographs by ANN E. YOW

FITZHENRY & WHITESIDE

This project (reference number 9596 OL-2/NL#01-1) was funded through the Adult Literacy Cost-Shared Program. This program is a partnership between the National Literacy Secretariat of Human Resources Development Canada and the Colleges and Program Planning Branch of the Post-Secondary Education Division of the BC Ministry of Education, Skills and Training. The partnership has been in place since 1987. The program has supported many innovative projects in British Columbia through partnership with community colleges and a wide range of community groups and organizations who have an interest in or are working directly in the adult literacy field.

For further information on adult literacy programs in British Columbia contact: Colleges and Programming Branch / Ministry of Education Skills and Training, PO Box 9177 / STN PROV GOVT / Victoria, British Columbia V8W 9H8 (telephone 250-387-6174)

For information on the programs of the National Literacy Secretariat contact: National Literacy Secretariat / Human Resources Development Canada, Ottawa, Ontario K1A 1K5 (telephone 613-953-5280)

Canadian Cataloguing in Publication Data

Main entry under title:
So far: words from learners

ISBN 1-55041-203-5

1. Readers for new literates. 2. Readers—Mentally handicapped—British Columbia—Interviews. 3. Readers—Mentally handicapped, Writings of the, Canadian (English). 4. Mentally handicapped, Writings of the, Canadian (English)—British Columbia. I. Bennett, Jean II. Jaccoma, Richard III. Weinstein, Lee IV. Yow, Ann E.

HV1552.3S6 1997 428'2 C97-900511-6

Printed and bound in Canada
Fitzhenry & Whiteside
195 Allstate Parkway
Markham, Ontario L3R 4T8

Book designed by Val Speidel

Distributed By:
Grass Roots Press
Toll Free: 1-888-303-3213
Fax: (780) 413-6582
Web Site: www.literacyservices.com

CONTENTS

ACKNOWLEDGEMENTS

The authors and editors of So Far *would like to acknowledge the following organizations and individuals who made this book possible:*

The Government of Canada's National Literacy Secretariat, British Columbia's Ministry of Education, Skills and Training, The Roeher Institute, The British Columbia Association for Community Living, School District # 36, Surrey, Open Learning Agency, Dr. Henry Amoroso, Libe Amram, Dr. Barbara Burnaby, Louie Ettling, F. Kazamek and Dr. Pat Rigg.

FOREWORD *by Lee Weinstein*

It is easy to find portrayals of the intellectually challenged in the mass media that range from the absurdly sentimental to the cruelly satiric. It is far more difficult to find forums that encourage intellectually challenged men and women to develop their literary abilities and express themselves in writing. Challenged adults often can't even get into literacy classes. And programs that do admit them, for whatever reason often end up occupying their time with busy-work.

The editors of *So Far* see things differently.

We began this project because we believed it would be exciting to create a stage for people who are rarely heard. *So Far* is one result of our work with a group of learners over the space of a year—interviewing, conducting one-on-one and group discussions, running a monthly writing workshop. The personal challenges our contributors face range from Downs Syndrome and brain injury, to cerebral palsy and other neurological conditions.

We think the result of our group's efforts, *So Far*, is an exciting document: Because with the exception of clearly delineated sections (this introduction, the short biographical sketches of each contributor) every word in this book was spoken or written by the learner-contributors.

Naturally, that is not to say all the writers' words are reproduced here verbatim. Just as we utilized the skills of a top-quality book designer and a remarkably gifted photographer in producing *So Far*, we also proofread every contributor's written and spoken words and cut them for length (a service given to most professional authors writing for publication).

It was, however, a point of editorial conscience for us that the vast majority of the words in this book would be those of the learners and the learners alone—and that while the text has been shortened and "tightened" editorially, their specific words in the interviews and writings are presented unchanged.

We believe *So Far* is remarkable in the creativity it has unleashed. But we hope it will not be unique. The themes in this book are universal: love, search for community, the struggle to overcome a lifetime of negative labelling and find meaning in one's existence. It is our deepest wish that other professionals who work with challenged adults and literacy learners will be inspired by what they see here not to replicate *So Far*—but to go far beyond it both in scope and quality.

In that spirit, here is a brief description of how *So Far* developed.

THE FUNDING

We applied for a "cost-shared" grant to Canada's National Literacy Secretariat and the British Columbia Ministry of Education, Skills and Training. In that grant we proposed to create a book based on the interviews and stories of intellectually challenged adults. Our stated goal was to give literacy programs something important, accessible and compelling for learners to read—and to influence administrators to see the challenged learners in their communities not as a liability to be avoided, but as students they wanted in their classrooms.

Fortunately, *So Far* encountered a wonderful—though rare—combination of circumstances: It was an idea for a product everyone agreed was needed—and our grant application was successful.

THE GROUP

We began recruiting individuals for the project by conducting interviews at the Invergarry Learning Centre in Surrey, British Columbia. Invergarry was a logical site because the Centre has been a leader in the field of literacy—and hasn't restricted access to literacy programs for challenged learners.

In the initial interviews, our main focus was to determine the important stories in each learner's life. Additionally—and most importantly—we explained the project as a writing workshop that would also produce a book. And we made it clear that not everyone chosen for the workshop would have his or her work published.

We also stressed that while the printed words would be the authors' own, decisions as to the actual stories and interviews used and the look of the finished book, would be the job of the editors and a professional production team—designer, photographer, creative consultant.

We began with a group of nine learners—seven from Invergarry and two associates of one of our editors from the community living movement—both people involved in self advocacy for a number of years.

Our criteria for selecting the group were based on which students and other individuals we knew who wanted to express their ideas using the written word, as well as our assessment of people's interest and commitment to the project. But speaking frankly, our decisions on participants were "editorial" as well: We made choices as to which people's stories were likely to create an interesting and effective editorial mix. It goes almost without saying that our final choices as to who would be included in the book were based even more strongly on this latter set of criteria.

THE INTERVIEWS

We arrived at Invergarry with tape recorder in hand, and conducted one-on-one interviews for up to one hour at a time with each person. Based on initial meetings, we developed questions about people's lives and interests that formed the framework for the actual interviews.

Once recorded, the interviews were transcribed and carefully edited for length and continuity. In printed form, they were shown and/or read to the participants.

During the course of the interviews, issues arose which went to the very heart of the project. Responsible editors must carefully weigh matters of legality, truthfulness and ethics in material selected for publication; and not everything that passes the test of human interest is automatically worthy of being printed.

One contributor wrote about taking part in a highly charged child custody case. The courts had yet to make a final determination as to the custody of the child. There were a number of issues which concerned us such as the safety of the writer, and protection of the child's identity, in addition to concerns about how publishing the story could affect a volatile situation. Although we believe the learner in question benefited from writing and speaking about a profoundly important matter, the interview and story remain unpublished.

Still another participant was ultimately dropped from the group towards the end of the interview stage. This was a student who was extremely uncomfortable with the interview format, and could not go beyond one-word responses to questions. Additionally, the learner's writing skills were low, making it impossible to tell a coherent story. We recognized the problem here was as much with our interviewing and teaching abilities as with the learner's responses, and believe that had there been time enough, the student could have told an important story. But because of limitations of time and funding, we stopped working together.

THE WRITING

The second stage of the process involved the writing workshops. There we talked about how to write the stories, about the importance of considering what to write before starting, and of needing to write several drafts to get a good final product.

Six of the eight participants, Barb, Gerry, Al, Margaret, Tony, and Burt were able to do drafts and final products which are published here. Two of the learners, Janice and Maxine, dictated stories to the editors.

Teachers who worked with the learners in their regular literacy classes reported how hard the students worked on their stories for this project: Students who had never written independently before, now wrote diligently during their free time at school. This alone demonstrates clearly how highly motivated people become when they are involved in a real publication that will be read by a real audience.

BOOK MAKING

We went over the edited interviews with each learner for a final time before we began the actual book production process. We asked if the interviews said what the participants felt was important, and if there was anything they wanted to add or delete. Some learners added information, but most were satisfied with what they had said and written.

We all met in late Spring prior to the production team's (editors, designer and photographer) first meeting to talk about what it meant to be published in a book, and about issues that might arise after publication—such as other people's reactions to what was said in print.Those learners who had been previously published had some negative experiences with associates and co-workers over their published pieces. We talked about the permanence of the written word and issues of jealousy, hurt feelings and how others can have different versions of the written story from the author. In the end all participants reaffirmed their commitment to remain in the book. We also talked about the photography process—and about the revealing nature of the kind of photography we would be using in the book.

Then we moved on to the actual production stage—and as with any professional publication, the process was essentially out of the authors' control. Publishing this kind of book for a wider audience is not an entirely collaborative process, nor was it ever envisioned as such. For example, learners did not have the opportunity to pick the photos they liked; nor did we put the book's graphic design, or its overall vision, up to a vote.

But we also knew that if the writers did not inform the content at every stage, the results would be counterfeit. And simply put, the making of a book is wonderfully exciting—we wanted everyone to witness and enjoy it. So as much as was humanly possible, all the participants were shown the progress at each stage, as *So Far* made its way from design to printing and binding. Most importantly, each author was shown his or her section at a late stage of the design process, and offered an opportunity for review and revision.

Although we have gone on at some length in this introduction, we trust the final product speaks for itself. Making this book has enriched everyone who took part in it. We know *So Far* is different and important. And we hope its usefulness in learning centers of all kinds is equal to the impact it has had on the lives of its learners and editors.

SO
FAR

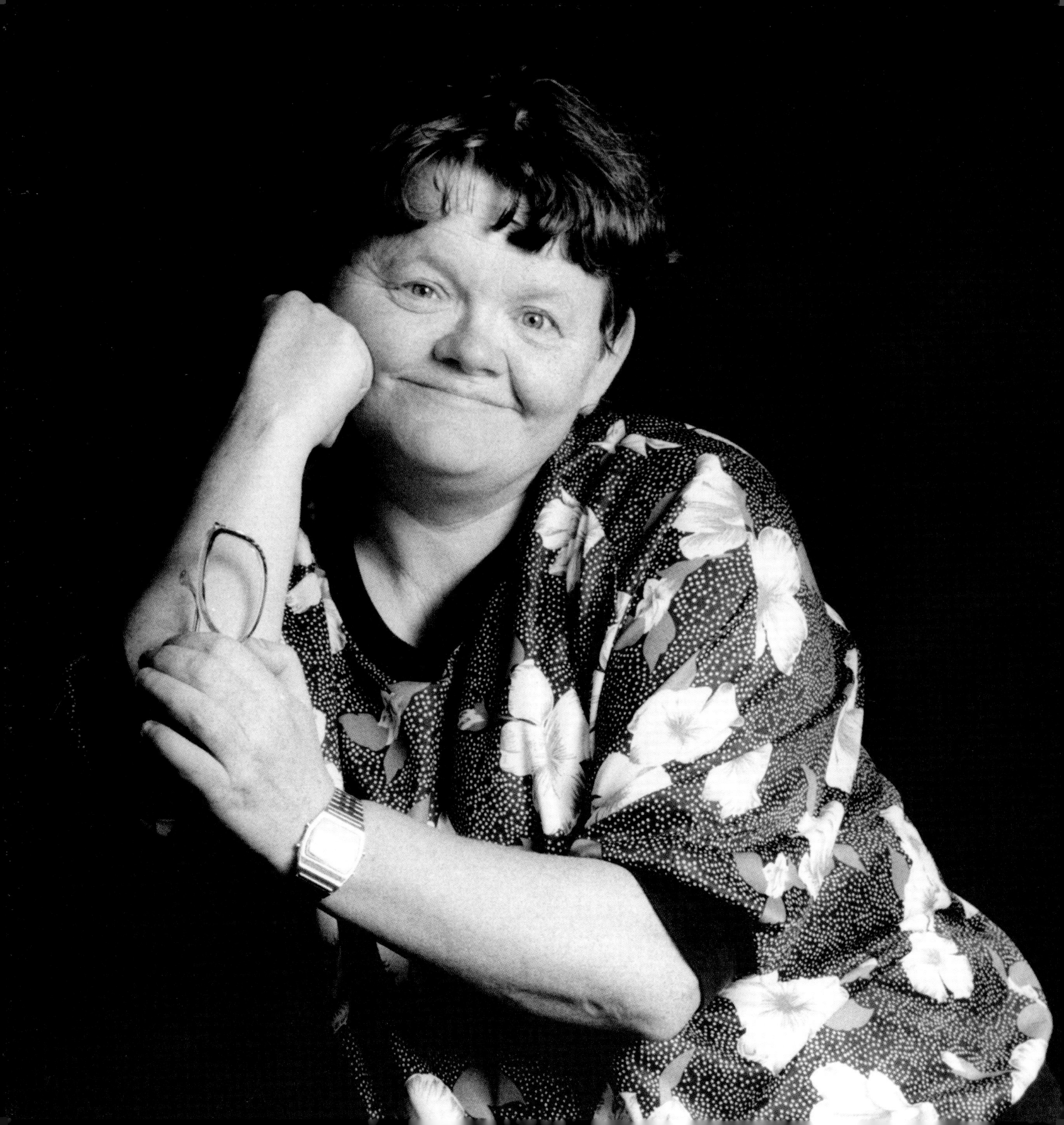

MARGARET MERCIER

Adopted at the age of 18 months, Margaret (51) spent her childhood on Prince Edward Island. From the time Margaret was a little girl she was told that she wasn't smart enough to learn how to read and write. Today, she knows that she can learn and that she has a lot to offer others. Margaret is passionate about the important role people at her church and at the Invergarry Learning Centre have played in supporting her and helping her believe in herself. Now, one of the most important things for her is sharing what she's learned with other people who have a hard time believing in themselves.

Margaret is an alcoholic, and has been sober for 13 years. When she's not involved with activities at her church or the Invergarry Learning Centre, Margaret likes to relax at home. She has her own apartment in a private home, but as Margaret describes it, the owner is more like a big sister to her than a landlady.

MARGARET'S STORY

I came to B.C. by going to bingo. My sister and my mother and I went to bingo one night. I only took 30 dollars and it was the last game. I had all my numbers covered and B9 was left. My sister told me it was covered, so I yelled "Bingo!" and won the game. But after I won I didn't know what to do. . . .

My girlfriend lived in B.C. and she was always writing and telling me to come out. I still didn't know whether I wanted to go out or not. I received a letter from her that day and she still wanted me to come out, so I came out. I'd won 500 dollars.

And how much did it take to come out to B.C.?
Just exactly 500 dollars. When I got here I couldn't find my friend. So I stayed in a hotel. I found my friend the next day. I didn't tell her I was coming. I surprised her. I turned up on her doorstep. I knew where she lived by the letters she wrote me.

What did she say?
Her eyes just popped out and she didn't know what to say! After me telling her I wasn't coming out, she was really surprised. I just said hello, and she stood there just looking at me. I came out to visit, but I ended up staying.

What made you decide to stay?
The weather, the different temperature. I'm still not used to the weather. The attitude of some people. The scenery. I come from a small village where there's no hustle and bustle. I was bewildered by the sounds and the scenery. I liked it. The friendly attitude . . . the people were like home. I could speak to them, talk to them, make them understand. Down where I was from, I couldn't do that. In B.C. I could make people understand who I am and where I was coming from, but down home I couldn't. Since I've been here I've learned to appreciate people and I've learned to appreciate myself a lot more than I used to. I know when I feel down, my friends will pick me up. They can sense it. I've got the kindness and the friendliness of the people. They're behind me; they don't tell me I can't do things. They taught me I shouldn't say no until I try. Then if I can't succeed, then I can say no. [Before] I always was saying no to everything.

Facing page: An enthusiastic student, Margaret grabs a cup of tea and sticks to the books while other students break for lunch.

Page 6: The New Westminster Union Gospel Mission is an important part of Margaret's life. She often rides the bus to the mission to socialize over meals and attend Bible study and worship services. The mission staff also helped her find the apartment she now calls home.

Page 7: Decorated with her collection of unicorns and teddy bears, this quiet, clean apartment is Margaret's dream come true. The suite is located in a private home and Margaret enjoys a close relationship with the family.

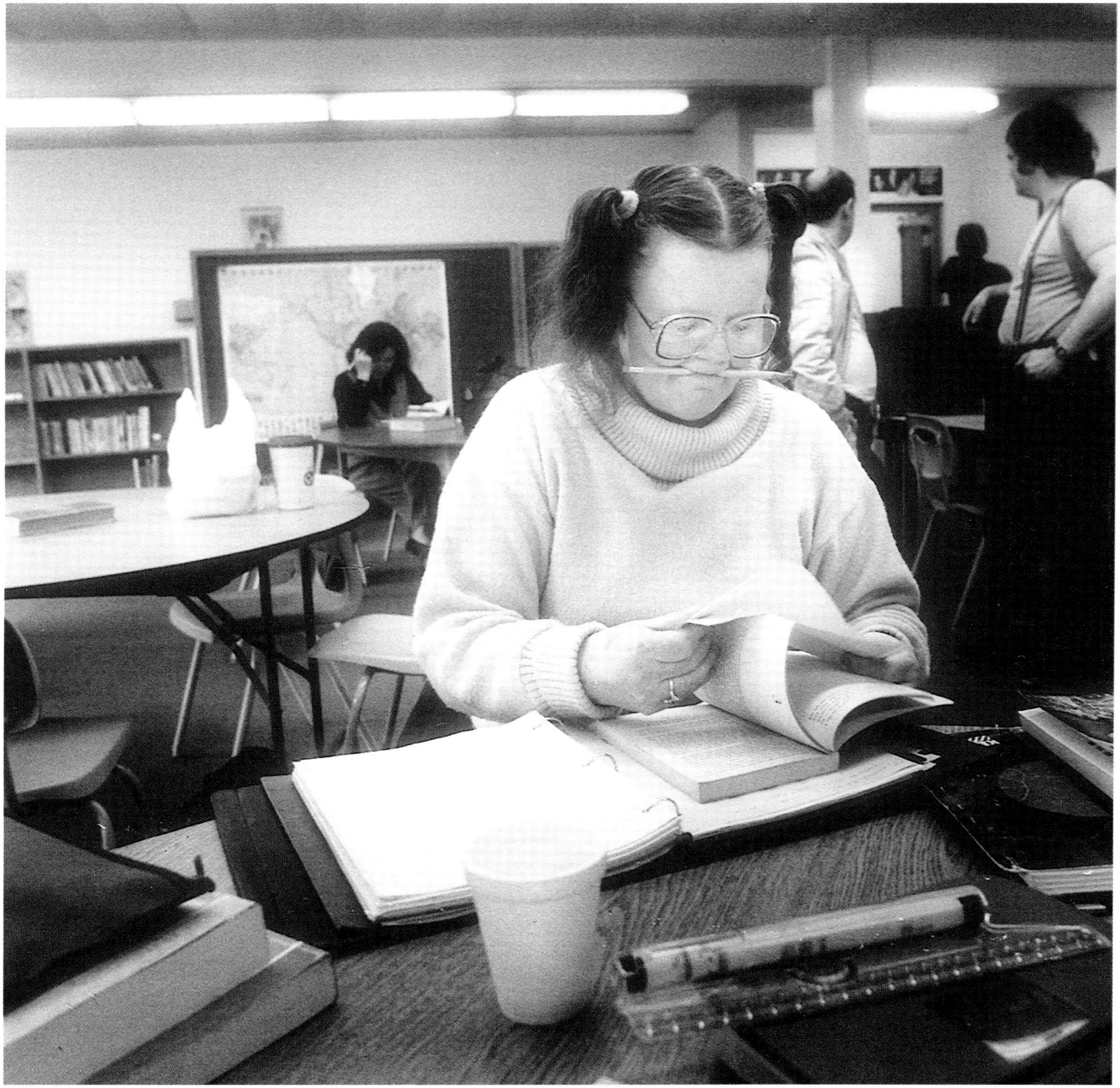

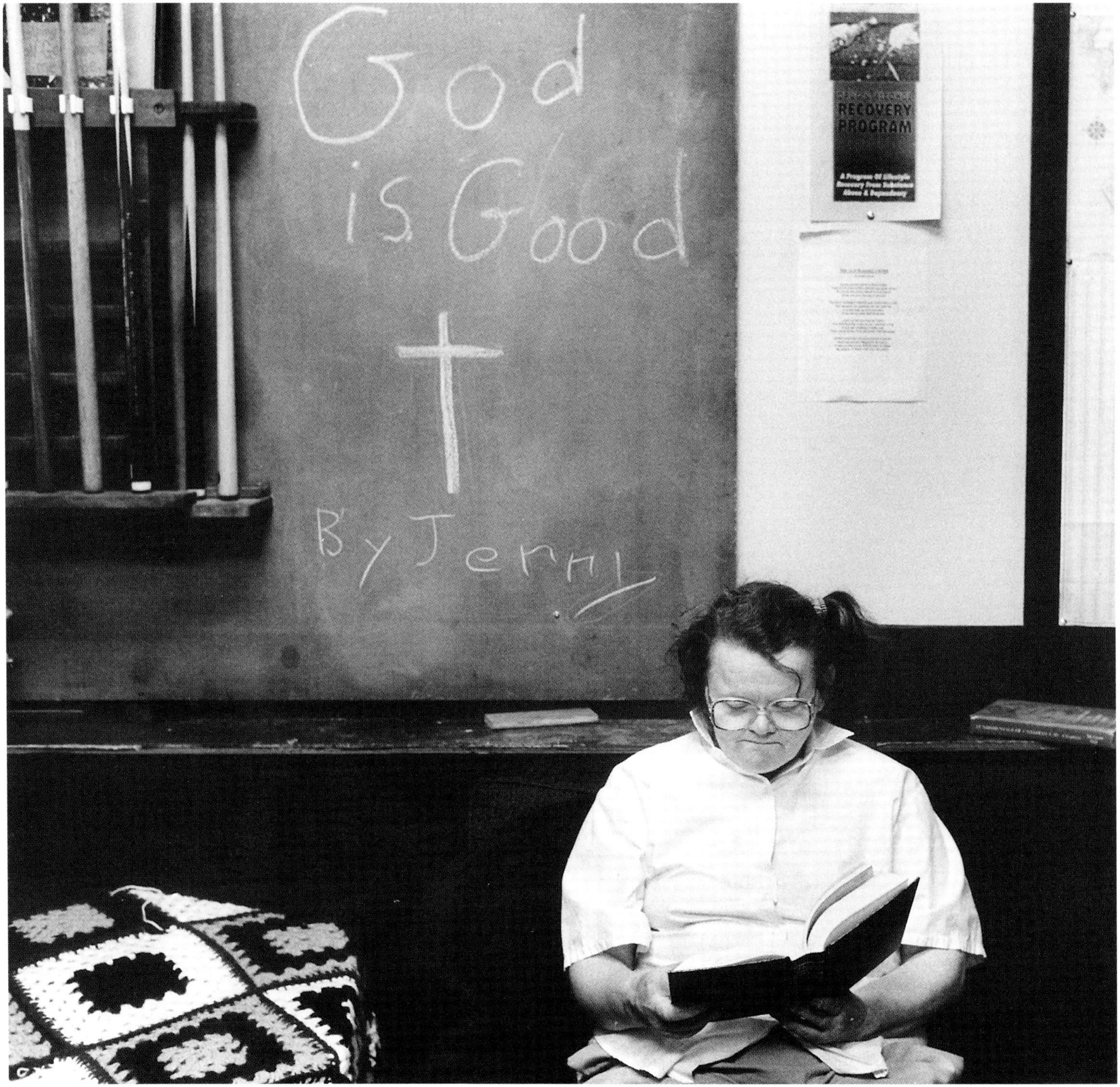
God
is Good
By Jerry
RECOVERY
PROGRAM

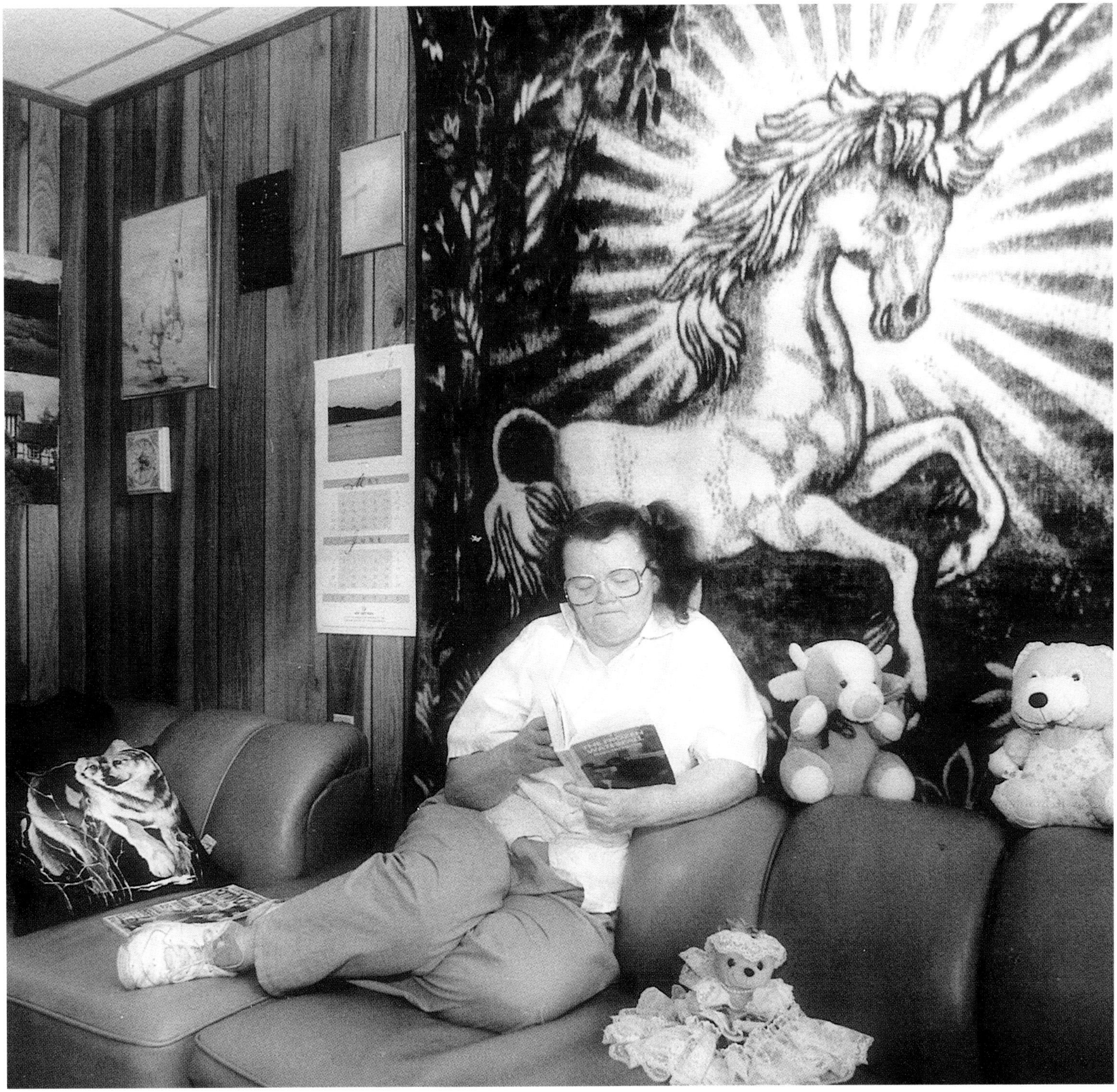

How was that different from what it was like back home?

Well, my parents had always told me that I was good for nothing and I could never do anything right. I never had support, so I never would want to try anything. But now I've made friends who tell me that I can do things, so it gives me confidence in myself. Before I came out here I didn't know who I was or where I was going or what I was doing. Now I know who I am and I know what I want and I know I can achieve it with the support of my friends, my school friends, the teachers, my church friends, and just ordinary people. Like my landlord. She's not my landlord, she's my big sister.

Like I have arthritis in my back and she's always concerned; like she wanted to come and pick me up at school. She didn't want me to be out in the rain. She's always concerned about me, where I never had it before. And it's kind of strange because before, when anybody wanted to do anything for me I always thought I had to pay them for it. But through my landlady I've learned that's not so, that there are people who care. It's genuine love for me; and I never had this before. It's kind of strange and I don't know how to accept it sometimes. I get upset a lot, but I know I shouldn't.

I'm that same way. Ever since I was a little girl, I always wanted to help other people, and I'm still like that. I remember my Mom getting mad at me because I used to come home with no shoes on, and she'd ask me where's my shoes. And I said I gave them away. And they used to be real expensive shoes. So she'd get mad at me.

My childhood wasn't that great; I had a stepfather who abused me and stuff like that. I had people tell me I could never do what I want. I grew up believing in that. But since I came to B.C. I have friends saying, "Yes, Margaret, you can do it," so I want to do it. I used to do things half way and then get this foggy notion that when people tried to help me they wanted something—so I would quit a job. Now I'm learning that's not right. If I want to achieve anything I can't quit.

I have a sign in one of my books that says, "You will succeed if you don't stop." Like if you want something, go after it and continue doing it. So this is what I want to do in my life. And I'm starting to believe in myself. Before, I lost that. Now I've found it and I'm doing something about it.

What did your Mom and your sister think about you heading off to B.C.?

Well, my children are out here, and I haven't seen them for a long time. That's another story. My mother was just concerned that I'd go out and push myself on my children, when they weren't used to having me around. And I said, "No, I won't do that." Other than that, she had the confidence in me and she didn't mind me going. She's another one who protected me from the hurt. She tried. But I learned later on in life that she was abused by my stepfather too. So there was nothing we could do; we couldn't help each other. But she's someone I love dearly.

You have four kids?
Two boys and two girls and now I'm a grandma. My boys had two boys and two girls. I'm very well pleased. I know where they are and everything but I don't want to push myself on them. Things from what happened in my past that they're not quite ready to accept yet. When they're ready they will come looking for me and ask questions and I'll be ready to answer them.

Tell me about what happened with your kids and how they ended up in B.C.?
Well me and my husband broke up because he was an alcoholic and he abused me so I left him. . . . Every time I wanted to talk to [my children] . . . he'd threaten me. I've told the kids that he'd threatened me and in order to save myself I had to stay away from them but they don't see it, they can't see, they just see why couldn't I be there. . . .

Your children came out here as adults. How did you end up reconnecting?
I knew before I came out here that they were out here because they used to write to their grandma, my Mom, so I knew they were out here by them writing to her when I was down home. She was able to keep in touch with them. She was by my side all through this ordeal from the start with the break up with my husband, to the end . . . to giving up my children.

It sounds like you have a different understanding now.
Like I said to my friend the other day, my father and I never got along. But now I have the understanding; and I wish he was here to see what I've been doing. I would like him to know that yes, I've got love in my heart for him. With all the abuse and the stuff . . . there was reasons. Today I believe in reasons. There's a reason for everything we do.

MARGARET'S WRITING

A NEW HOME

When I finally decided to leave Prince Edward Island my sister and her daughter took me to the bus station in Charlottetown. As we boarded the car ferry to cross the Northumberland Strait to Nova Scotia, I looked out the window at the red soil disappearing in the night.

As we traveled, we stopped in Halifax, Nova Scotia. I met a nice young gentleman who was traveling to British Columbia too. I had brought a radio with me to pass the time away. As we traveled, we heard on the radio that a man had stolen a bus from a small town and set it on fire. When we had gone a fair distance we saw the frame of the bus.

I remember coming in to New Westminster and being very surprised to see such big mountains. Where I come from in Prince Edward Island we don't have any mountains. I couldn't realize why there was snow on the top and not the bottom. So I asked a little old lady why.

It was late when we arrived in New Westminster at the bus stop. I told my friend on the bus that I had Rosemary's address, so I was going to take a taxi to her house. He told me he wasn't leaving me until I found Rosemary. I told the taxi driver her address and he took my friend and me to the wrong address. The person I got out of bed at three thirty was not very pleased.

Then we went and were lucky to find a hotel at that time of night. My friend said good-bye to me at the door. It was refreshing to sit in the bathtub. I could not sleep very well my first night in a new city. The new noises were very strange to me. The cars and buses were very fast and people were in a hurry to go everywhere so I thought.

The next day I took another taxi to my friend's house. When Rosemary saw me she didn't know who I was for a while. Her eyes were like footballs. When she realized who I was she gave me a big hug. Then she made me one of her stupendous meals. We stayed up talking and reminiscing about our friendship together.

The scenery was very surprising because there were things that were not on PEI. When I went to Stanley Park for the first time, I thought the flowers were very beautiful. They were from all over the world. It was hard for me to get used to the ever-changing weather. The people's attitudes were different.

That is why I came to visit in 1983 and why I stayed.

Facing page: A surprise visit to old friend, Rosemary Muise in 1983, marked the start of a new life in Vancouver for Margaret. The two friends share long conversations over coffee, pinochle games, and walks in the park. "I know when I feel down, my friends will pick me up," says Margaret.

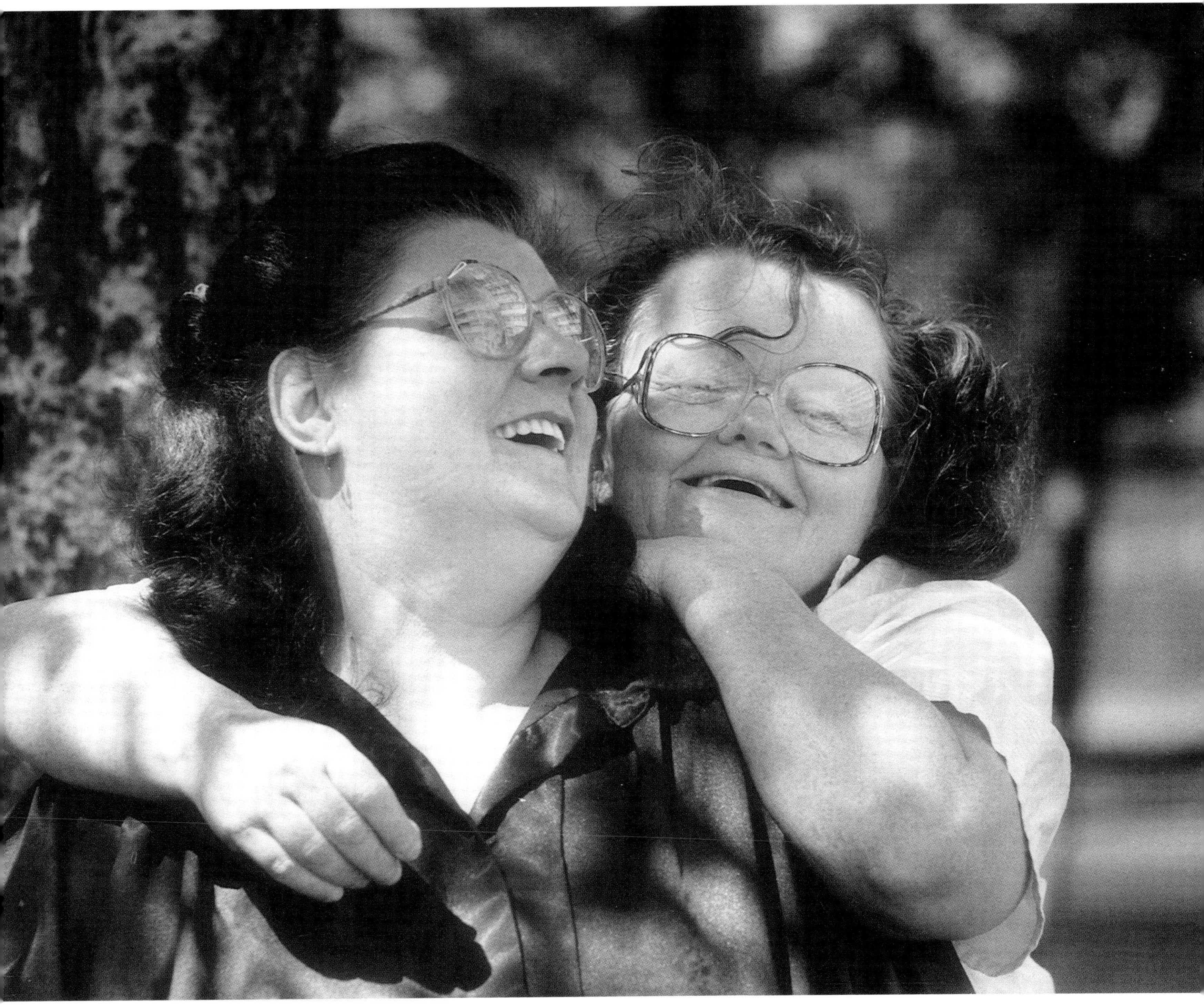

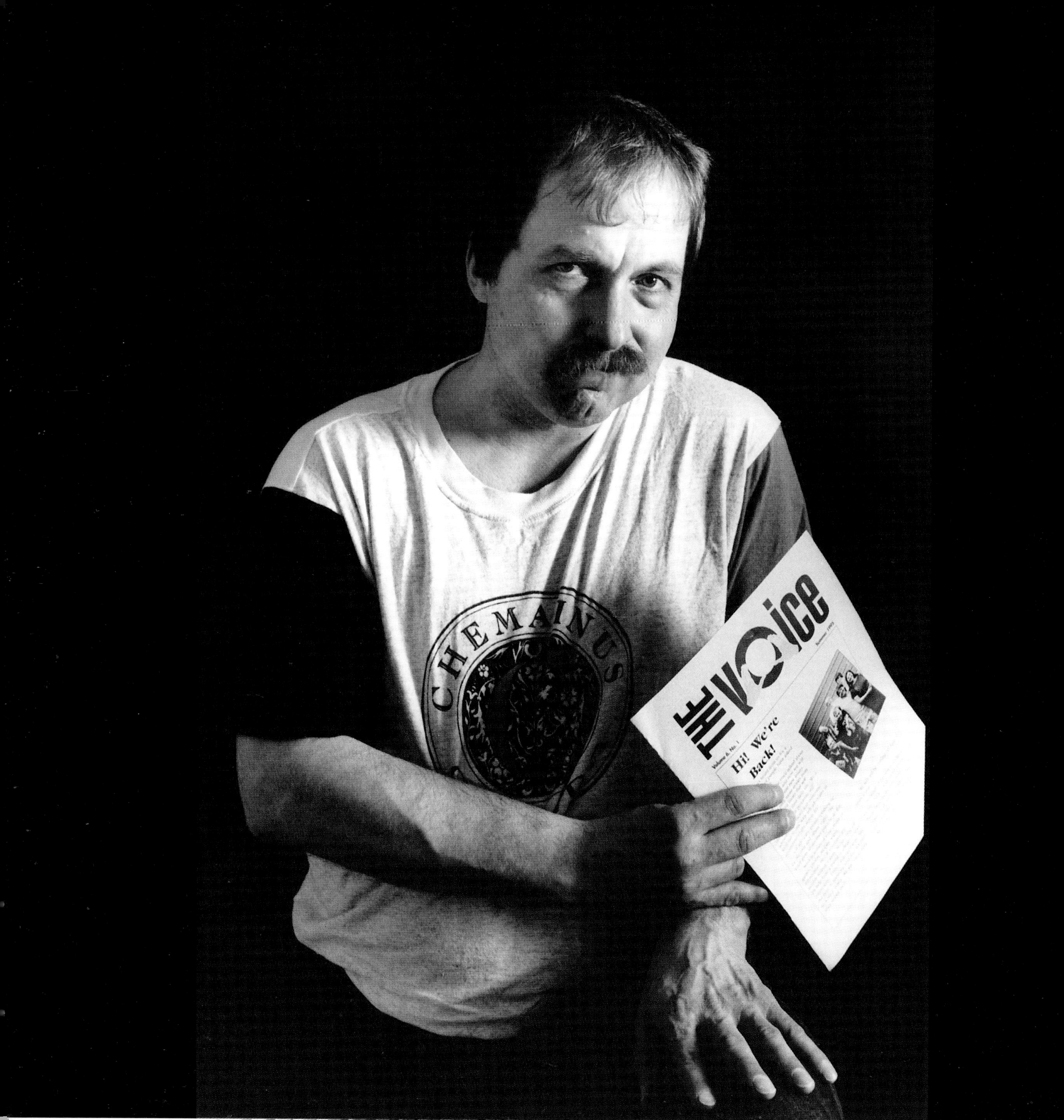
CHEMAINUS
THE Voice
Hi! We're Back!

GERRY JUZENAS

Gerry (43) worked for 8 years in his church's workshop, the last 3 years as an assistant supervisor. Recently, Gerry lost his job when funding for the workshop ended. Though he misses the people, his life is full with other activities.

Gerry is in demand as a speaker and seminar leader for groups who want to learn more about self advocacy. He also chairs the Self Advocacy Caucus of the B.C. Association for Community Living and helps produce *The Voice*, a newsletter written by and for self advocates. Gerry is particularly proud of his work with *The Voice*, which he helped found in 1988.

Gerry loves to travel. He has been on trips throughout Canada and the U.S. and hopes to travel in other parts of the world in the future. When he's not at meetings or traveling, he spends his time listening to his large collection of rock and roll music. He borrows CDs from the local library because he can't afford to buy all the CDs he would like to have. One of his hobbies is writing out the words to favourite songs.

About three years ago, Gerry reconnected with his step brother who he hadn't seen in many years. Since then, he has met many other family members. But the part he likes the best is being an uncle.

GERRY'S STORY

You wanted to talk about your Mom and the things going on in your life up till the time that your Mom died.

Well the first thing about when she died . . . it was quite a shock to me, because she was a very young lady at the time. I was only a teenager and she was about 35 years old; very, very young. I was in school, and I got a call to come into the principal's office. When I heard she died it just totally shocked me. They said, "You better go home; the rest of the family will explain it to you better if you don't understand." I got home and my grandma told me. I'm not sure where my Dad was at the time—can't remember that far back. I didn't know anything of what a heart attack was. They told me how she died. She was by herself . . . and boom . . . she had a heart attack, didn't regain consciousness. It just happened so fast. In those days they didn't have the proper things to get somebody to recover. Today, they have all the equipment.

What was your Mom like?

Well . . . when I think of mothers today in society . . . I'm really lucky to have had a very good Mom. She treated me like a human being. She always gave me things . . . We always had family gatherings . . . I always enjoyed trying my best to celebrate her birthday, too. We had good times. If I wasn't sure what was going on all the time, I could talk to her, in case I didn't understand things.

She was someone you could go to if you were confused or upset?

That's right. And I loved her a lot, of course.

So what happened in your life after she died?

Well, basically it was okay for a couple of years. But then something happened. I had no friends. . . . It started me for some reason to drink alcohol. The first couple of times I drank . . . I didn't know it was getting to me . . . I just drank basically by myself. After I finished high school my Dad had a business. Things were going really bad there; I was drinking there, I was having relationship problems with my father and some of the people in the business. And later on, when I left . . . my attitude got worse. I was basically just yelling for no reason at all. . . . And my alcohol desire was really a behavior problem. Then somebody started me to join my first meeting.

Facing page: Gerry and girlfriend, Wendy Menzies, spend a summer afternoon in a local park. "I never thought I could be this happy again in my life," he says.

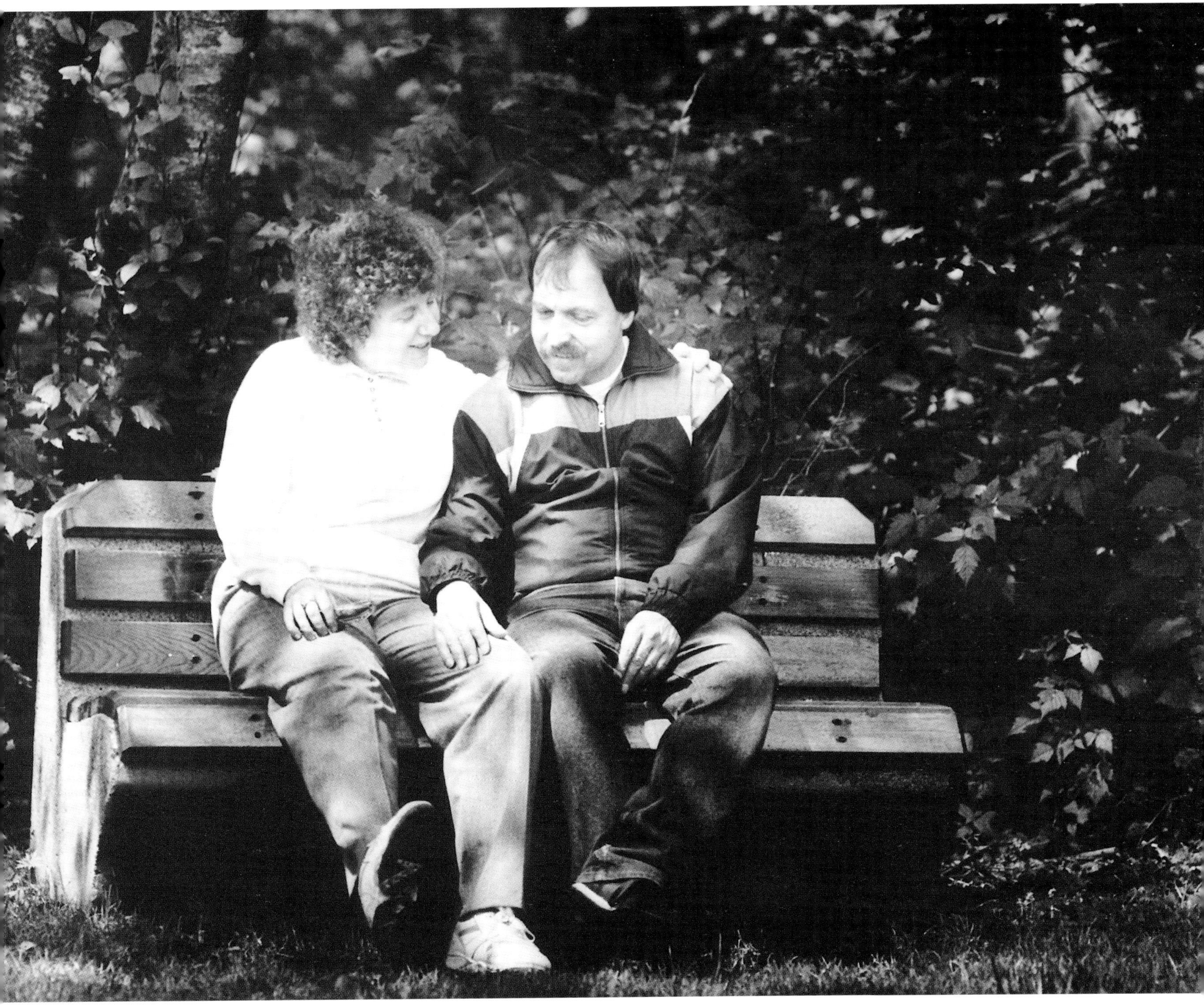

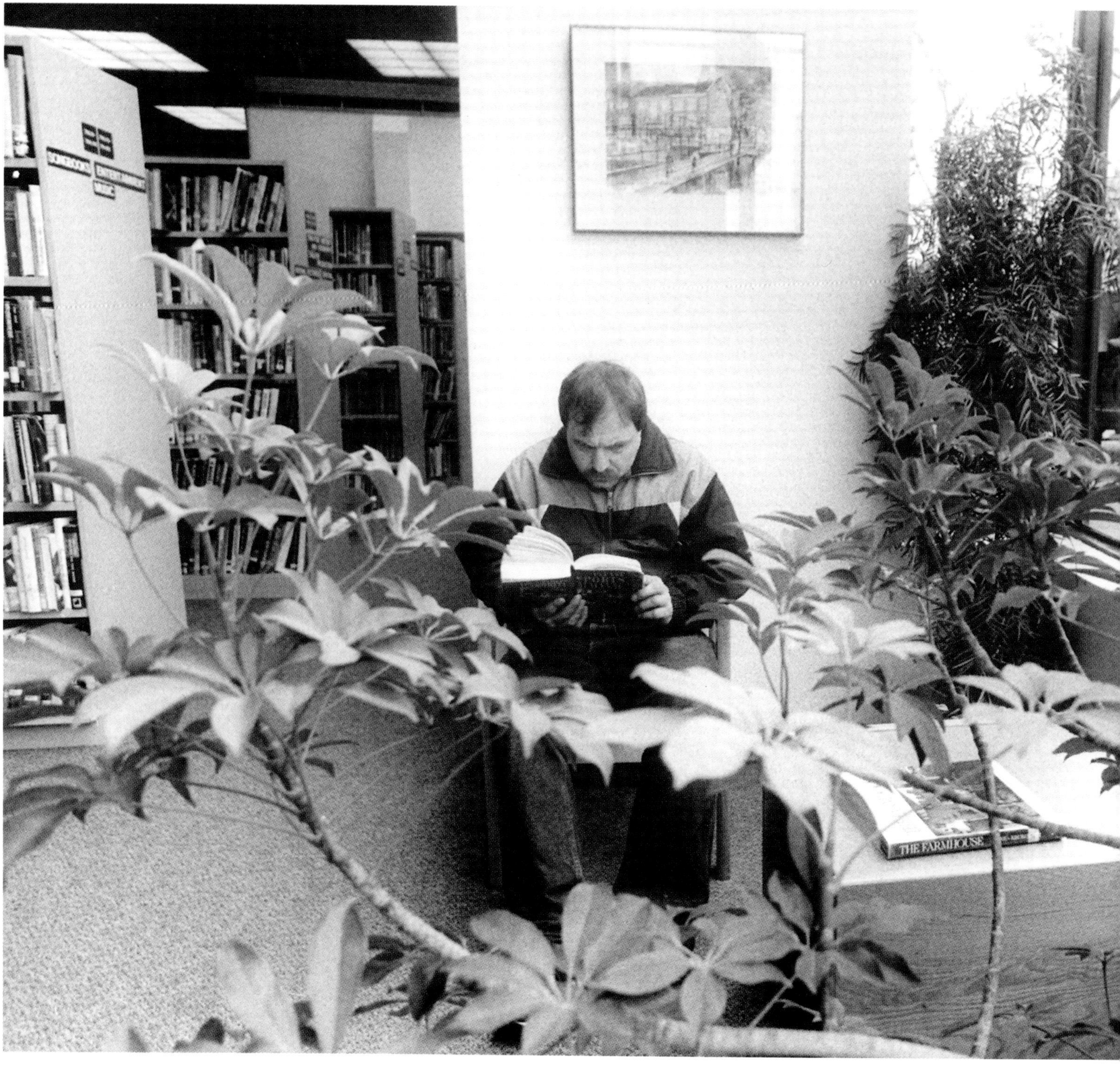
SONGBOOKS
ENTERTAINMENT
MUSIC
THE FARMHOUSE

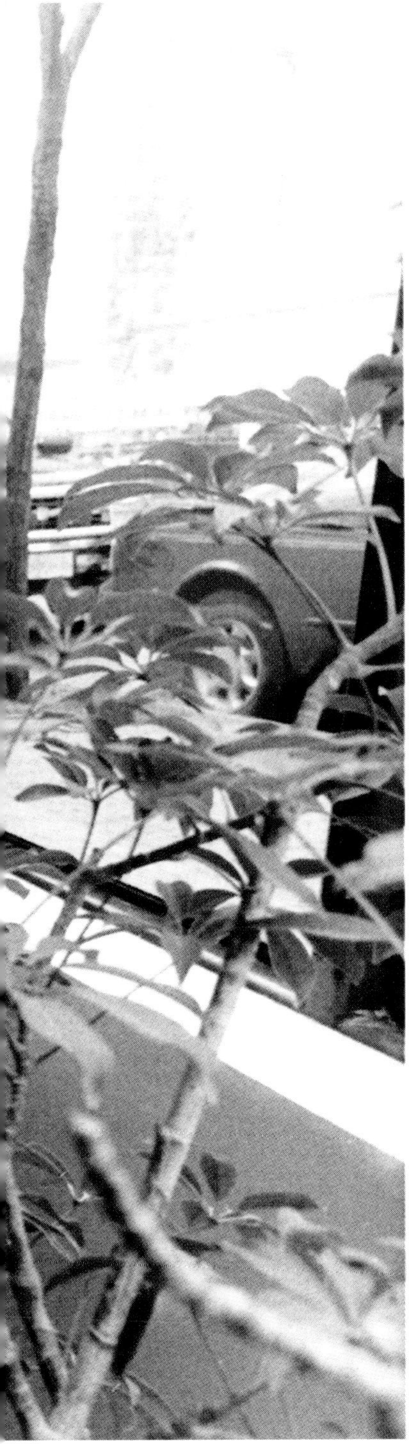

What kind of meeting was it?
Well, it was a group of people, a group called People First. I was asked to join that group. So I said, well, maybe I can try this. I gave in to anything people asked me. So I gave in to that.

Were you still drinking?
Yes, I was. I would give in to anybody who asked me to do things, or the opposite way, when I was still drinking I would give in the wrong way. I would give them a "no" for no reason.

You didn't know what you wanted?
That's right. And I didn't know anything about how to express my feelings.

Is this one of the times that you really felt your Mom's absence?
It began to hit me later on, when my Dad changed too. We were falling apart. Either I was making a mistake and he was getting after me; or I was yelling at him. But then later on . . . I just basically went down into my room and I just got shy.

What enabled you to get off alcohol?
Two years of being in my first group. . . . I was the president . . . they asked would you like to meet some more people . . . so I said okay, I gave them "yes" as usual. Later on, I disappeared for awhile. Then I decided to get some professional help. I said, "I need help right now." I felt it. As soon as I got that help, my life began to change more.

Was the professional help counseling?
A psychologist—like a doctor more than a counselor. I learned how I can change, how I

Gerry finds a quiet corner for reading on his weekly visit to the library.

can treat people better. Now, I know pretty well how to say yes to things and no to things, too.

What difference has all of that made in your life?
Especially for the last five years . . . I feel really good. . . . For example, I was doing my first project, to get *The Voice* started, a self-advocate newspaper. Soon as I got a process in there, I got comfortable, I got friendly, my attitude changed completely. Then later on when I was picked to go to the conference for BCACL (the British Columbia Association for Community Living). It was just a new thing and I said, "Oh wow, there's a good new step for my life. Maybe I can try something, just absorb and see what it's like to have a big association and see what self-advocate outfits do out there." So I went to their caucus. I found out a whole history about them. . . .

Are you still involved with The Voice?
Yes, and I'm one of the original people still there. I'm so proud to be on that. It makes me feel good inside. We've got a new format now. We're giving people a chance to write stories to show their lives, and we connect ours with them as well. I think it's really important. I enjoy that, and I've kept every copy.

If you were able to talk to your Mom, what would you want to say to her?
To tell her how much I've changed. To explain what a self-advocate is. How much I'm involved with it. To tell her I'm a clean man . . . I don't mind telling her about my drinking problem and that I'm being sober. To tell her I have a nice girl in my life now. . . . I would tell her about all my trips. . . . My best adventure of all was going on a trip across Canada and part of the States last year by plane and by bus tour. I went through New Brunswick, Prince Edward Island, Nova Scotia, Quebec City, parts of Ontario. In the States I went to Maine. . . . I saved up money and it was something I wanted to do for myself, just to show you can do something to celebrate, and have the best time of your life.

And Mom. . . ? I love you.

A big fan of rock and roll and country-western music, Gerry browses the library's collection of CDs for new titles.

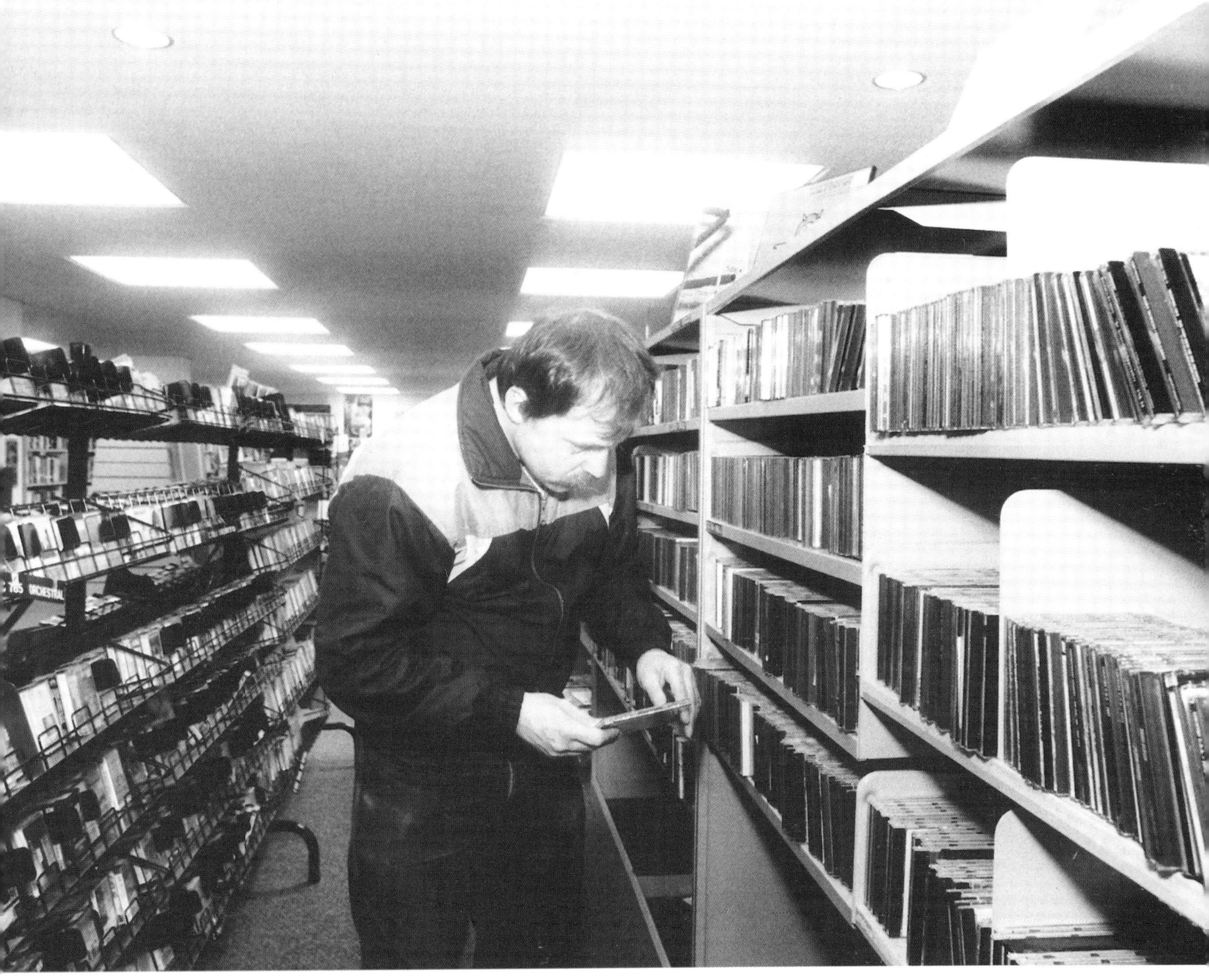

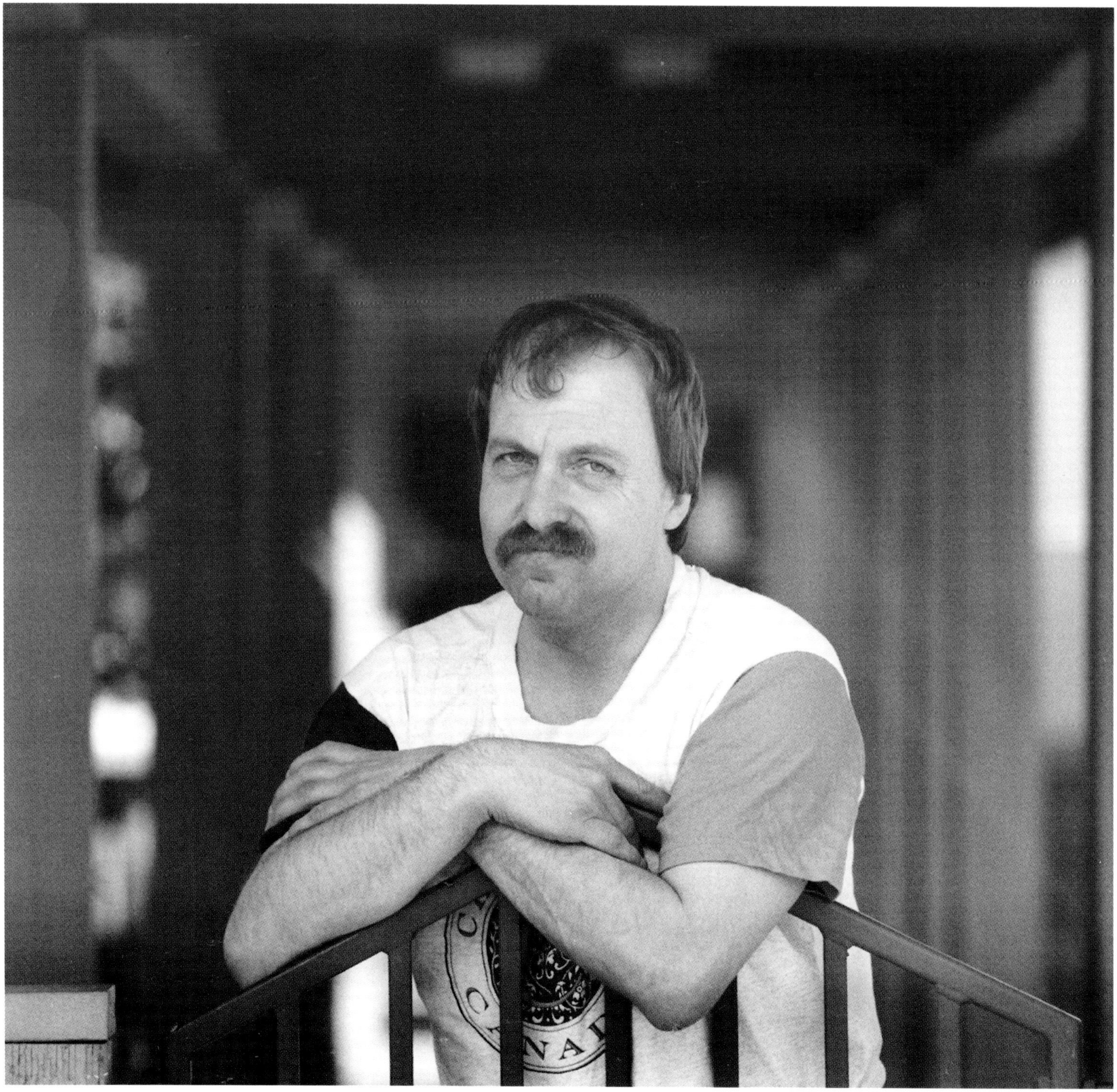

GERRY'S WRITING

GERRY'S LETTER TO HIS MOM

Mom,
I'd like to tell what my life is today. When I was drinking I didn't know how to say no. Afraid of losing friends. When had a problem with my Dad, didn't talk about it or express my feelings. I found out that I had brain damage when I was born. I wanted to have a girlfriend but didn't know what to do—no one taught me about how to be in a relationship. I had a bad attitude like getting mad at my friends, finding out that I was handicapped. Not getting along with my Dad—what could I do to make him feel better and make up with him and forgive him too?

Mom, I have changed. I haven't had a drink of alcohol for about eleven years now. Also now I know how to keep my friends and know how to have relationships with women. And, I have forgiven my Dad. I want to tell you too, that I'm involved with Lower Mainland Based Community Service where I am the president and I'm a Director-at-large at British Columbia Association for Community Living. I have been on the Self Advocacy Caucus for 5 years. I have also been on many trips.

All of this I told you so you can be glad and proud of me too.

Facing page: Gerry has lived at Filby Court for over four years. He enjoys having his own apartment and has added another recliner to his living room for television dates with girlfriend, Wendy.

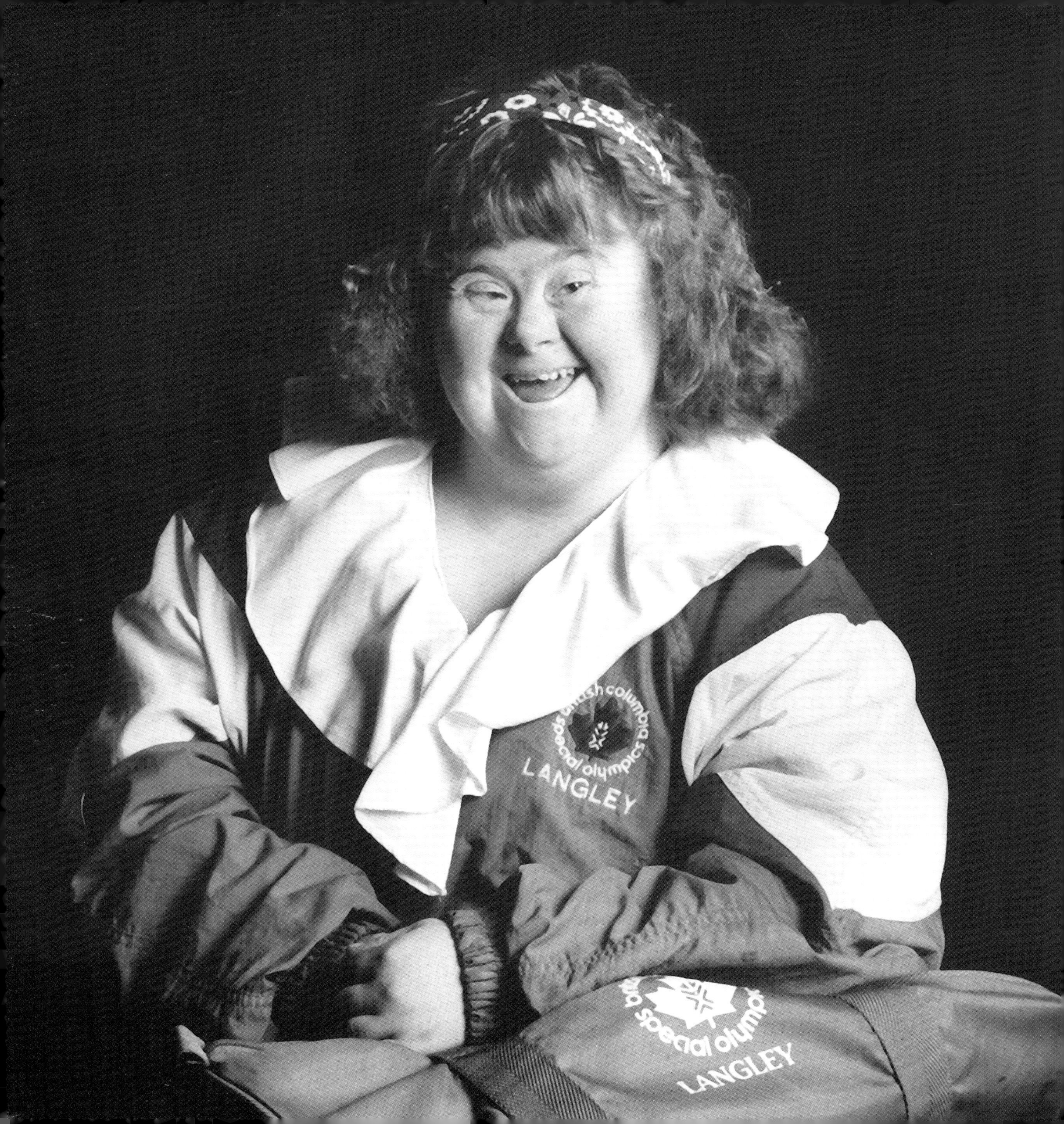
british columbia
special olympics
LANGLEY
special olympics
LANGLEY

MAXINE MACLEOD

Maxine (29) has been through a lot of changes in the past few years. After living with her Mom most of her life, about three years ago she moved into a group home. A year later, her Mom died. Then, a few months ago she moved into an apartment she shares with a roommate who helps her out with things she's not sure about. Among Maxine's other important relationships: She was recently going out with Al Waddell, whom she met at the Special Olympics. She met Wade, her current boyfriend, at their group home.

Her dog Daisy, a black and white Boston Terrier, lives with her Dad. Maxine couldn't take Daisy with her when she went into the group home. Now, she doesn't get to see Daisy very often because her Dad lives so far away. When Maxine lived with her Mom, they used to take Daisy out for walks every day. Maxine still misses those times, especially the walks with her Mom. On Mother's Day she puts flowers on her mother's grave.

In addition to spending time with Wade, her boyfriend, Maxine works at a Salvation Army store three afternoons each week and attends gymnastics, dance, and track and field classes. She has an extremely gentle manner, and a strikingly soft, musical tone to her voice. Maxine has been coming to the Invergarry Learning Centre for a year and is enjoying learning to read and write and understand numbers.

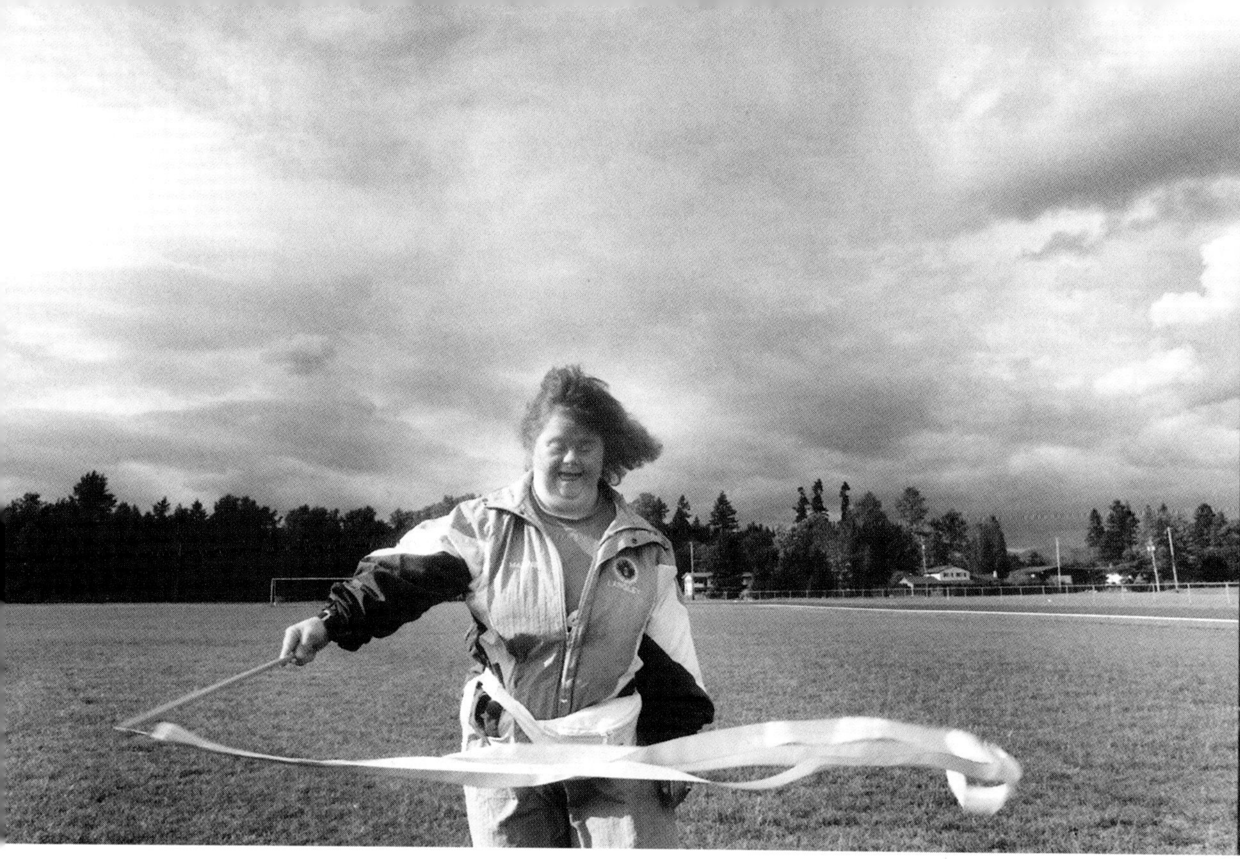

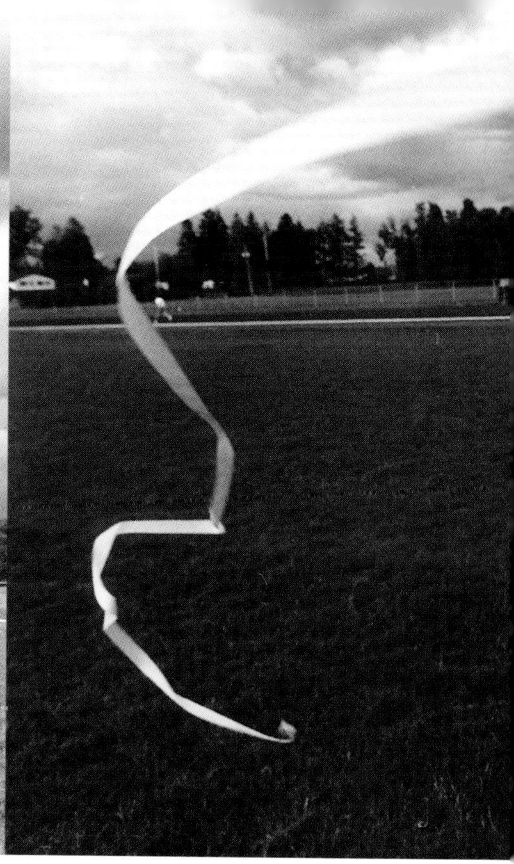

MAXINE'S STORY

First Interview: Maxine and Al

How did you and Al get together?
We met at the Summer Games. He saw me at the Games. Then we met on the dance floor and he asked me to go on a date and I said yes.

What did you think of Al when you first met him?
He's kind of cute. I went to his house for dinner.

Did he make dinner?
Oh yes.

Does he cook well?
Oh yes. He does.

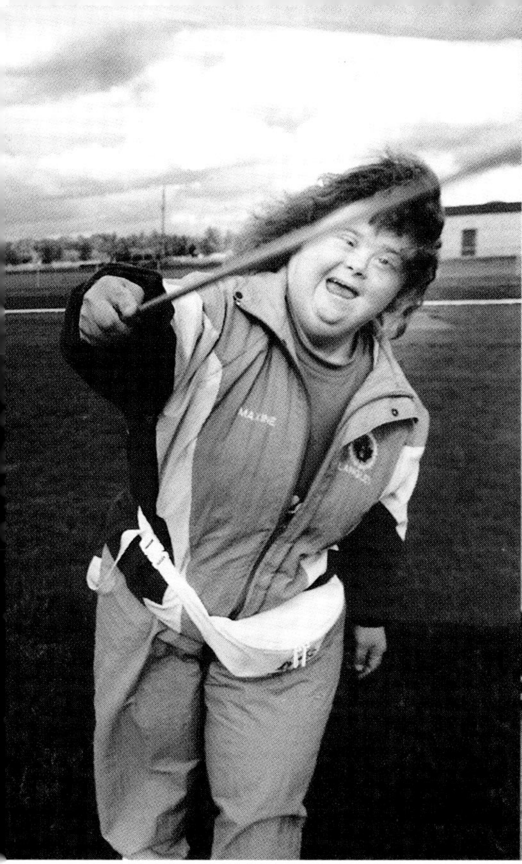 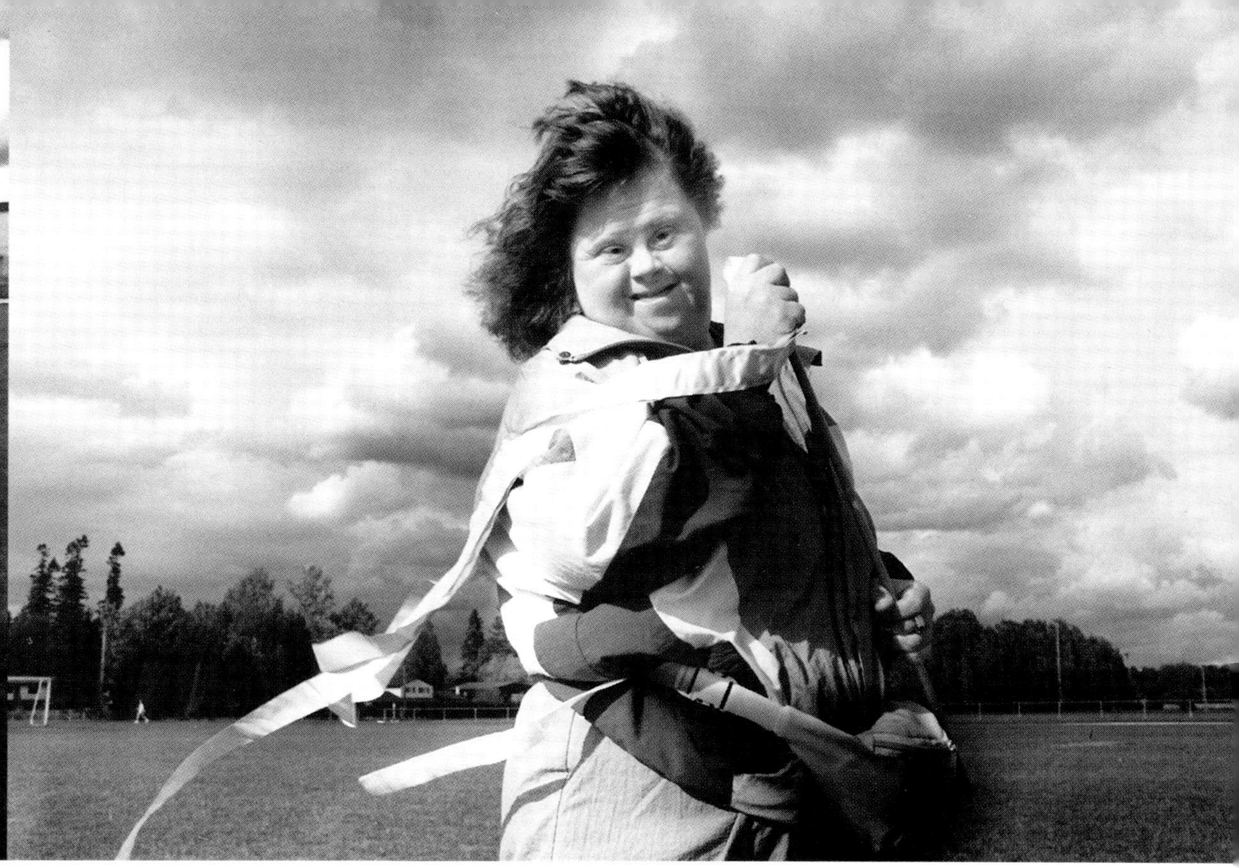

What does he cook?
Chicken . . . potatoes . . . corn . . . beans . . . noodles . . . steaks.

Do you ever do the cooking?
Sometimes he wants me to do it. I say yes. He likes my cooking.

What kinds of things do you and Al do together?
We go out for dinner. Sometimes we go to the mall to look around and he buys me coffee.

And you guys got engaged?
Well, I'd got engaged before then. And he was engaged before.

An active participant in Special Olympics, Maxine excels in rhythmic gymnastics. Her bedroom wall is covered with ribbons won during competitions.

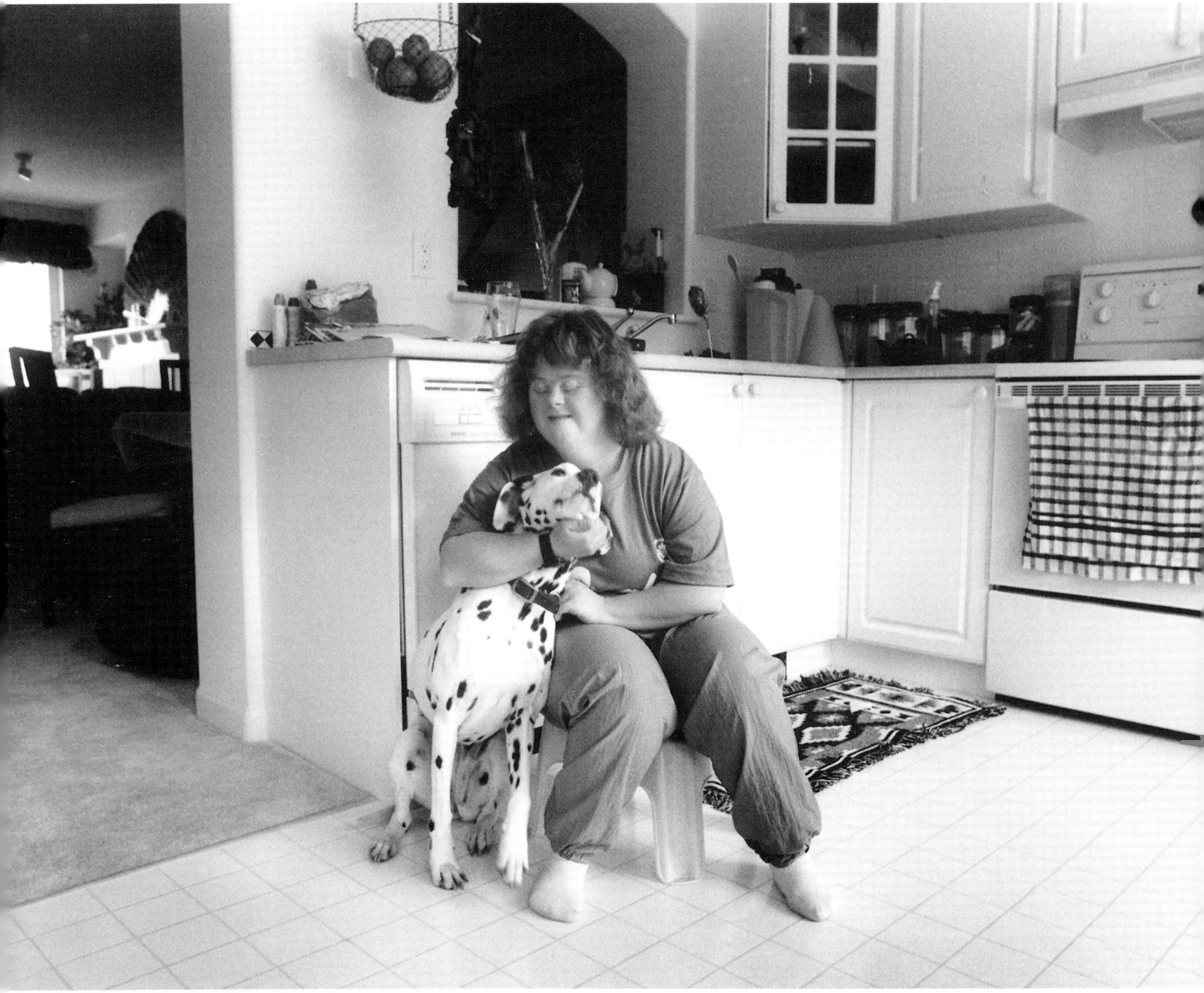

What did you think when Al asked you to get engaged?
He asked me at swimming. He said, "Maxine, will you be my fiancee?" I said, "Yes."

What did it mean to you to be someone's fiancee?
I love you . . . He's so nice . . . He tells me I'm pretty.

It makes you feel really good about yourself?
I'm so quiet.

And now you're talking about getting married?
I'm thinking about that. After I move out.

Out of your group home?
Yes. Not this Christmas. Next Christmas.

What does your family think about your plan to get married?
My Mom's not around. She's dead. I loved her . . . I liked to go for walks with her . . . I liked to talk to her. I miss her. I did some cooking around her . . . cleaned up the house. I'm glad I have my Dad. He's got a new place. I have a dog whose name is Daisy. Sometimes I feed my own dog.

What does your Dad think about your plan to get married?
He says that's up to me.

In the last little while you and Al have been having some harder times. Can you talk about that?
Well, my brother picked me up from school Thursday, he sat me down to have a talk. He said I'm not ready to get engaged yet. We have to be friends.

You and Al?
Yes.

What do you think of that?
I have to lose weight. The gym class is helping me to lose weight.

Facing page: The black and white decor of the townhouse Maxine shares with roommate, Stacey, is even repeated in Stacey's pet Dalmation, Katy.

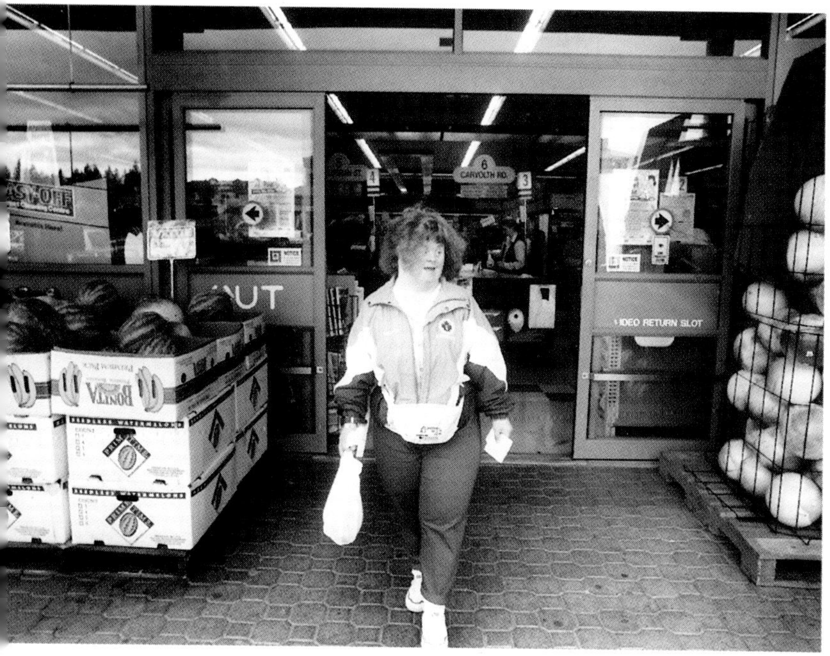

So your brother thinks that you've got enough things to work on with trying to lose weight. Do you agree with him?
Yes.

So how has that affected your relationship with Al?
I like it that way. He asks me to come over and spend the night. I can go there once a week, on the weekends. Sometimes I sleep with him.

Yes. That's a thing adults do. You're pretty happy about your relationship with Al?
That's right.

But you're also okay with not being engaged. Did you break off the engagement?
No. . . . I broke up the engagement, yes. Because I'm not ready. After I'm grown, I'm ready.

You just decided you needed more time?
Yes.

While Stacey does the shopping for main meals, Maxine decides on cold cuts for lunch during a quick trip to the shopping center next to her apartment complex.

Facing page: In addition to school and sports practice, Maxine works weekends at a local Salvation Army thrift store where she sorts and organizes merchandise (*inset*). She tries on a fringed jacket that caught her eye.

Tell us some things about yourself. What kinds of things did you do when you lived in the group home?
I had to clean up the group home. I had to do the vacuuming, change my sheets.

How long did you live there?
About six months.

And before that you lived with your Mom?
Yes, and my sister.

Did you move in after your Mom died?
No, this is before. My Mom took me to the group home. That's what I wanted to do.

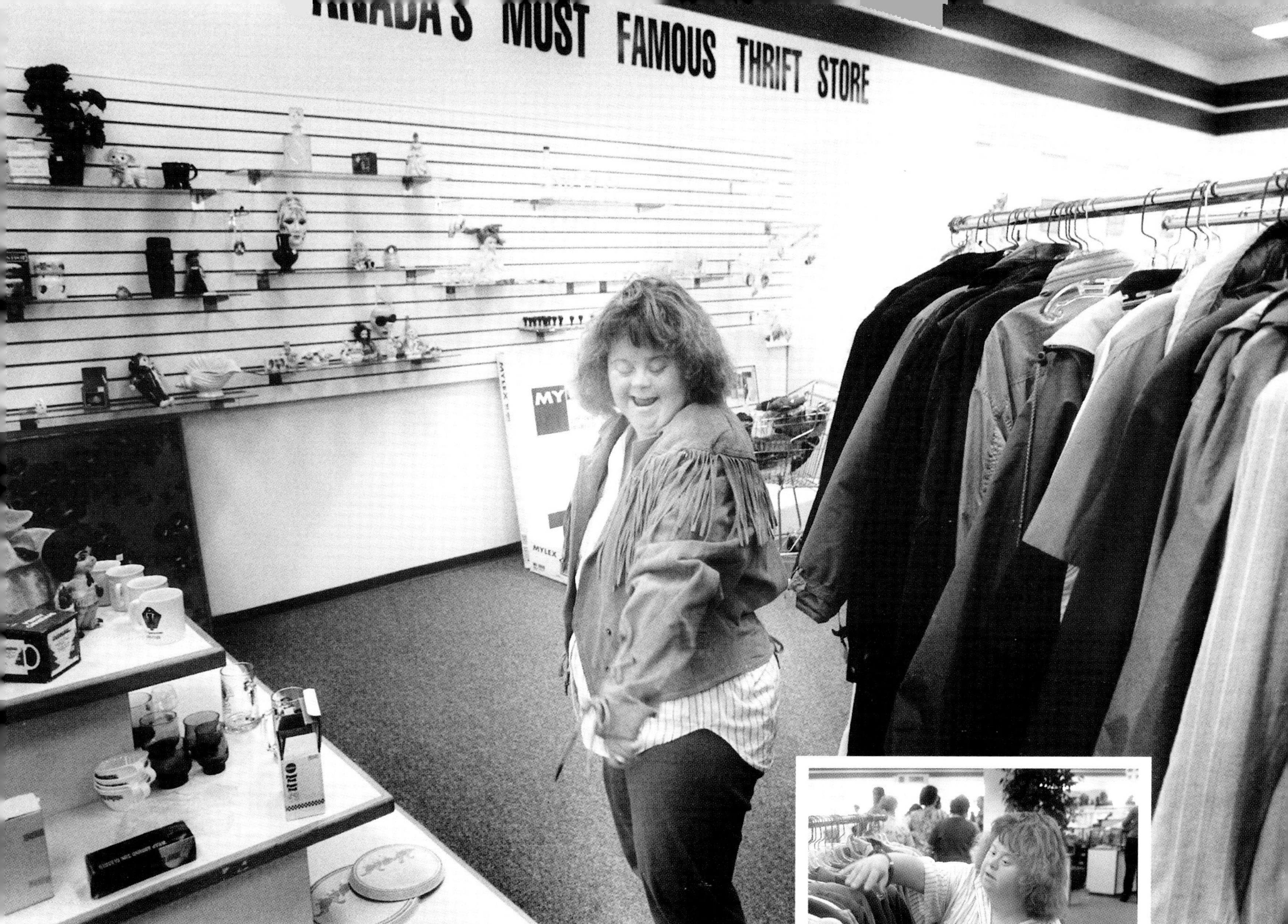
MOST FAMOUS THRIFT STORE
MYLEX

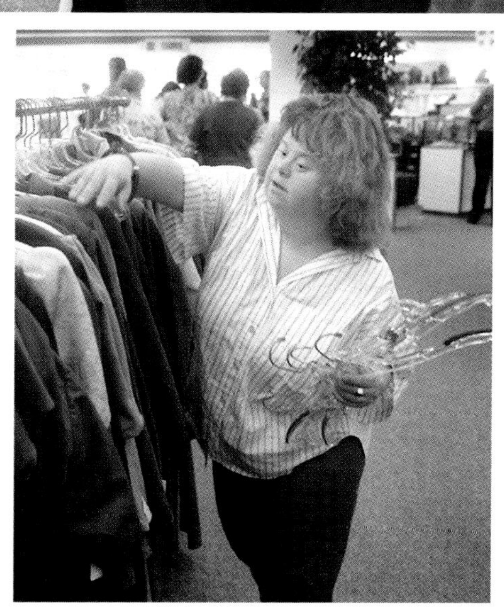

Second Interview: Maxine and Wade

You said you wanted to talk about your new boyfriend. How did you meet?
He moved in to my address, the group home.

So, you both live in the same house and that's how you met. What attracted you to Wade?
He was trying to make up with me, do lots of stuff with me. He likes to take me out for dinner or something or the movies. Going to the mall, play some games.

Do you and Wade spend lots of time together?
Yes, downstairs. Sometimes I go to his room.

Tell us more about what you like about Wade.
He's sweet and he's cute. His parents like me a lot. I go to his family's for dinner. I was there for dinner with them. We sat by the fireplace. We have a pop or something and he wants to kiss. He kissed me . . . He likes to cuddle up. I like to hug him. He's trying to be a very nice guy.

When we talk about him you know your whole face glows.
He makes me happy. He makes me laugh. I like it when he's teasing me. I like his face. He's a very nice guy. He's good looking.

Sounds like a really nice relationship for you. How does being in the relationship make you feel about yourself?
I feel good. Cause I like to be with him.

It's obvious that being with him makes you feel good about yourself.
Yes, 'cause I do all the activities. I go to gymnastics . . . bowling with him. I like to bowl on the same team as him.

Has your brother met Wade?
Yes. My sister likes Wade better than Al.

Does that make it easier for you?
Yes.

MAXINE'S WRITING

Winding down a day at Invergarry Learning Centre, Maxine works to organize word cards into complete sentences.

MAXINE AND WADE

He is nice. I like the way he dresses. I like to touch his face.
He's got nice soft skin and round glasses. I love him.

Sometimes I see him a lot. Sometimes I see him at bowling.
He comes to track and field. He goes to soccer.
He goes to floor hockey.

I like to go out with him. I like to go out for supper
or to a show or something.

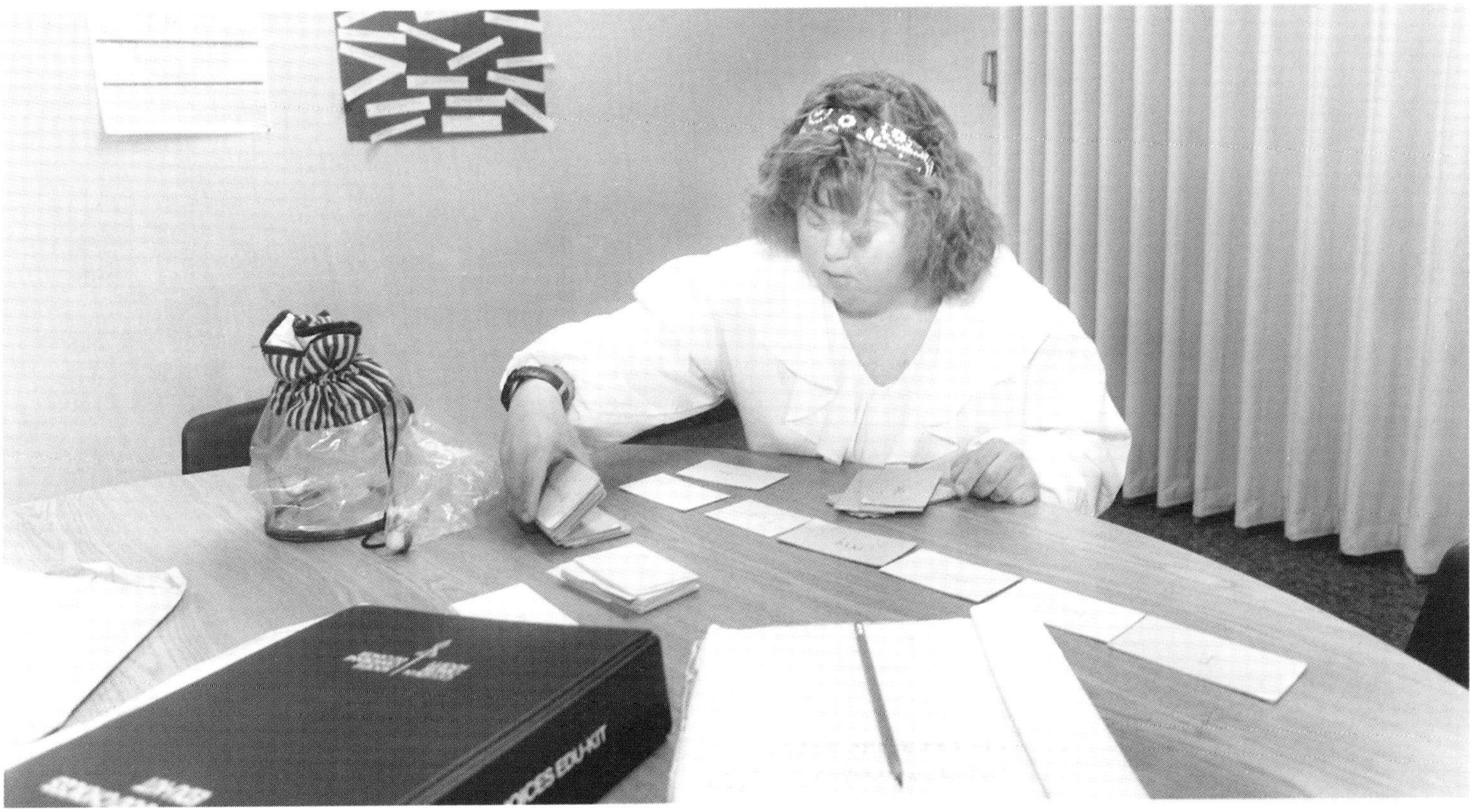

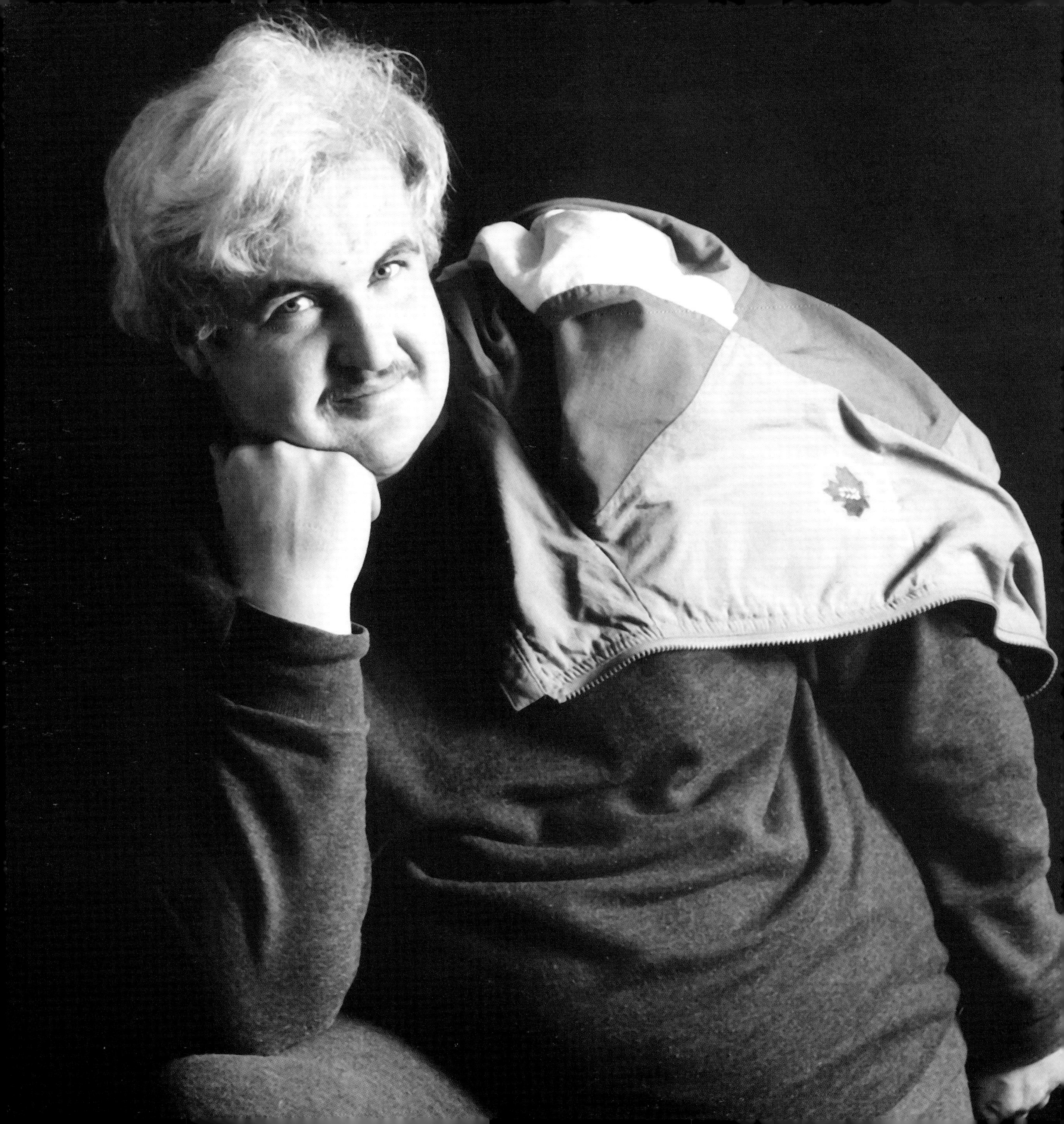

AL WADDELL

Al (35) say his big passion in life is Special Olympics. He participates in lots of different events depending on the season, and he's won many ribbons and trophies. Al met his former girlfriend, Maxine Macleod, through Special Olympics. We interviewed Al during the time his relationship with Maxine was ending. Al has a job doing maintenance and security at his apartment building. He fixes things that get broken, steam cleans rugs, and checks the building at night to make sure nothing is wrong. He's had lots of different jobs in the past. It's important to Al to keep himself busy with lots of work. Two of Al's hobbies are collecting hats and pull-tabs.

Al has a foster son he met through Special Olympics. His son is about 14. He usually goes to Al's place on Monday nights and they hang out and watch TV. Al has been coming to the Invergarry Learning Centre since 1984. He enjoys writing.

AL'S STORY

I first met Maxine about two years ago on the bus—with the other fiance she used to go out with. . . . She'd give me looks all the time like she had a crush on me. Then in Summer [Special Olympics] Games I saw Maxine doing her gymnastics . . . ribbon stuff. She saw me. . . . She was kind of shocked that she saw me there at the Summer Games, because she hadn't seen me for a long time. Then in July we were having a special dance for all the people. I danced with one girl, then I saw Maxine . . . and I danced with her—and I asked her out right on the dance floor. She said yes, and we started going out. As soon as I came back from Surrey I phoned her. She was staying at her sister's. I asked Maxine to go swimming. After, I took her out for supper . . . and we hit it off really smoothly.

What attracted you to Maxine?
I care about her a lot and she cares about me. I do like her a lot. We have our ups and down. Her Mom passed away . . . this year . . . and that's when she had to go into a group home. . . . It has kind of changed our relationship. There's one person there, this Wade guy, I don't like him. He's trying to steal my fiancee away from me. Ain't going to happen.

Have there been other changes since Maxine went into the group home?
It's kind of hard to explain. Before her Mom died, she used to live in Guilford and I lived in Surrey. Now I don't. I live in Langley, to be closer with her. And she doesn't have to travel back and forth.

How has the relationship changed your life?
I try to help her and she tries to help me. But she's trying to change my life around. Sometimes . . . well . . . Jesus. . . .

She tells me to change my attitude. Well, *her* attitude is not good. Sometimes I say bad words—and sometimes she calls me bad words. She started hitting me around—and that's no-no-no. Sometimes I get really grumpy at her. We just talked about it—how I feel. And she hardly does that anymore. She's got her own keys for my place. And I don't know when she's going to be moving in with me.

Facing page: Winning scores in Special Olympics bowling competitions have earned Al armloads of trophies which line his window sill.

Pages 35–36: After school and work, Al settles in for an afternoon of Nintendo which he says he can play for hours. An avid music fan, he also makes his own tapes which are scattered all over his apartment.

Are you going to be moving in together before or after you get married?
Before that. She wanted to move in with me . . . in the worst way. I feel good. . . . Spend more time with her.

What kinds of things do you do together?
We go out for supper; to the movies. Sometimes her and I go to the bar and have a couple of drinks. Sometimes we'll dance there.

You like dancing?
Ah, yes.

If you were going to write a letter to Maxine, what would you say?
I would say . . . 'Dear Maxine, "Roses are red, violets are blue, How sweet she will be . . ." '

So you'd like to write her some poetry. Would you say anything else in your letter?
'I want you to be my wife.'

You're really looking forward to being married.
Yes. Trying not to be nervous. This is my first time. And first time for her.

What kinds of things are you nervous about?
If she wants to get married to me. I know she loves to. . . .

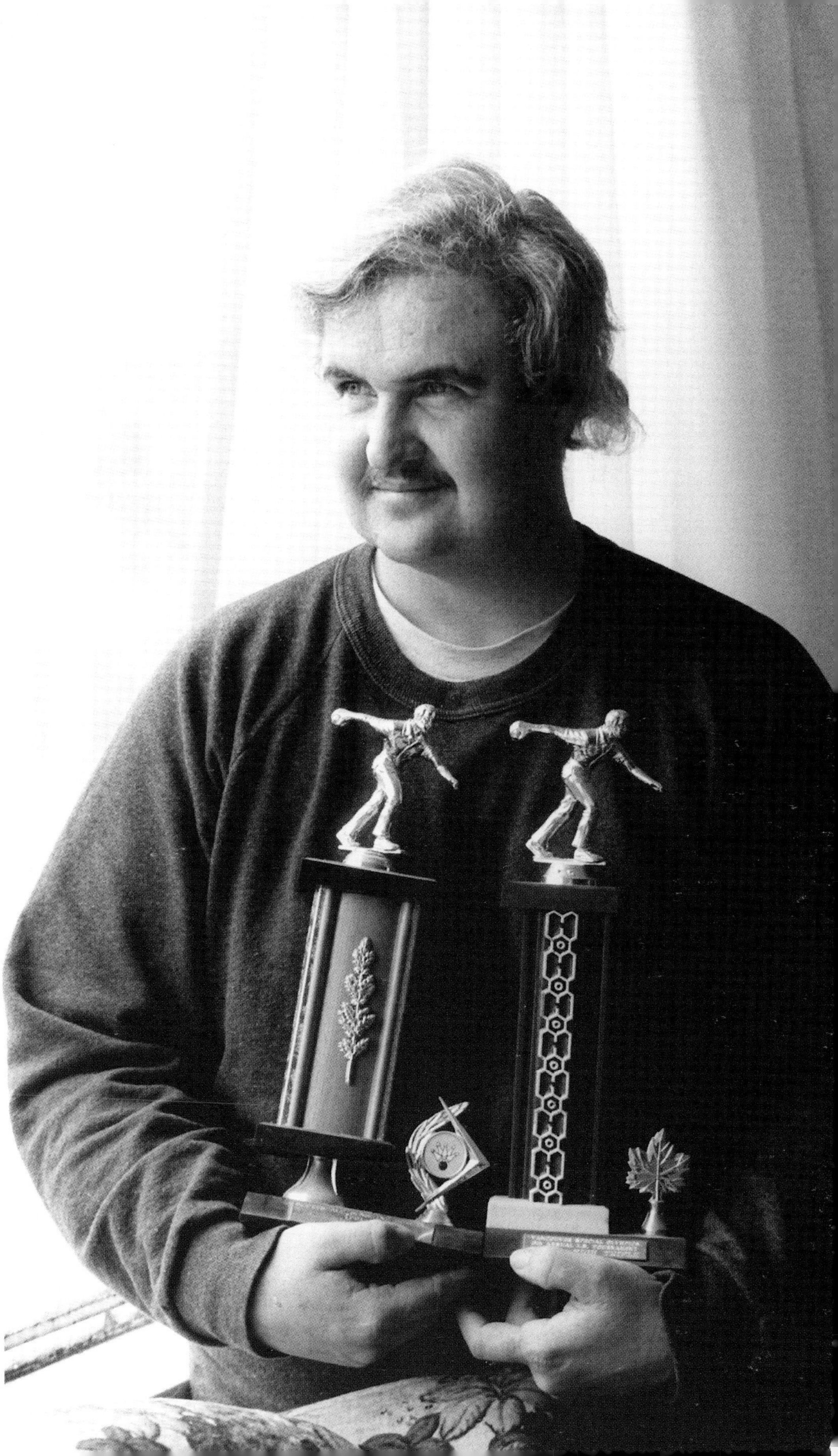

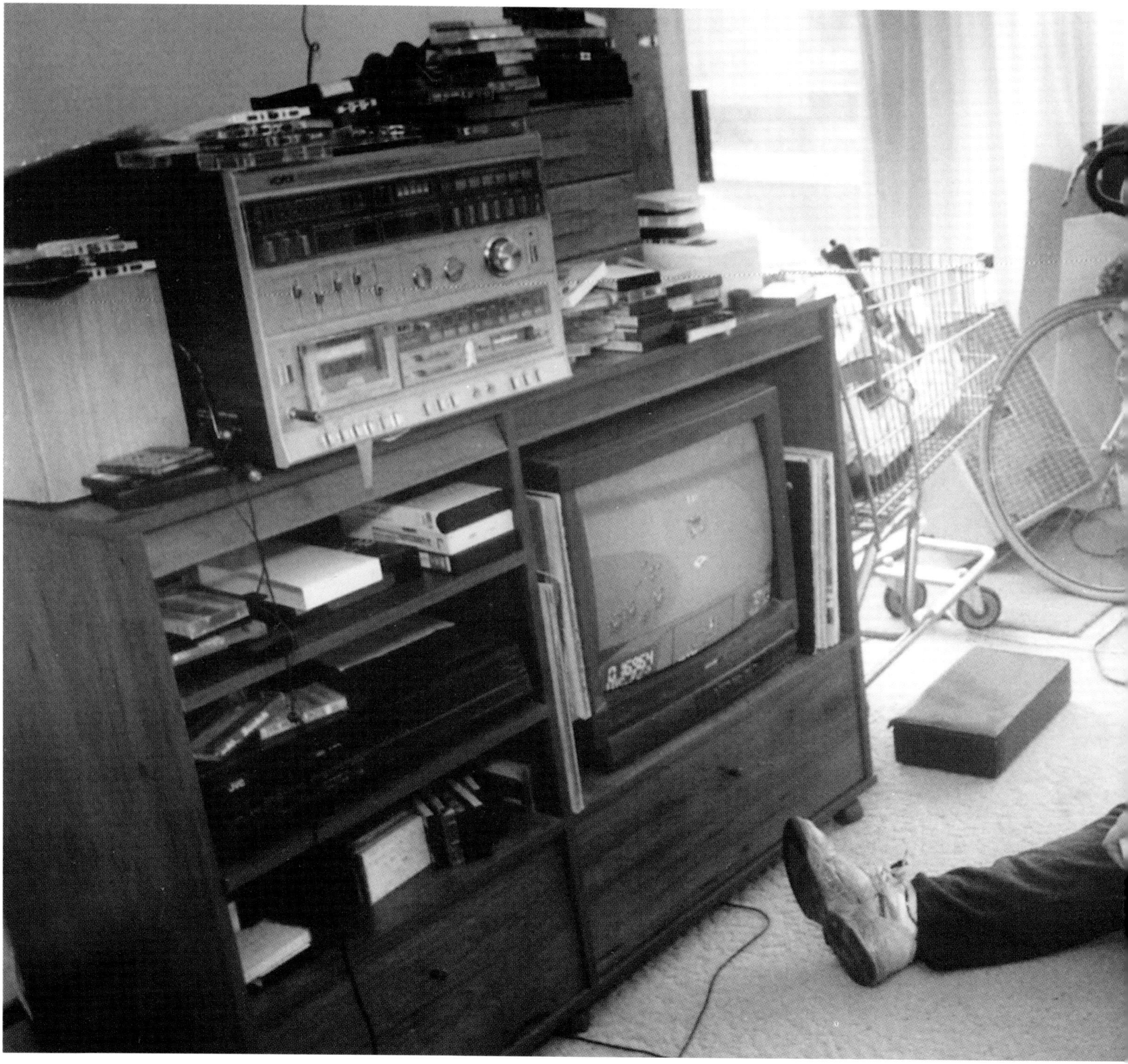

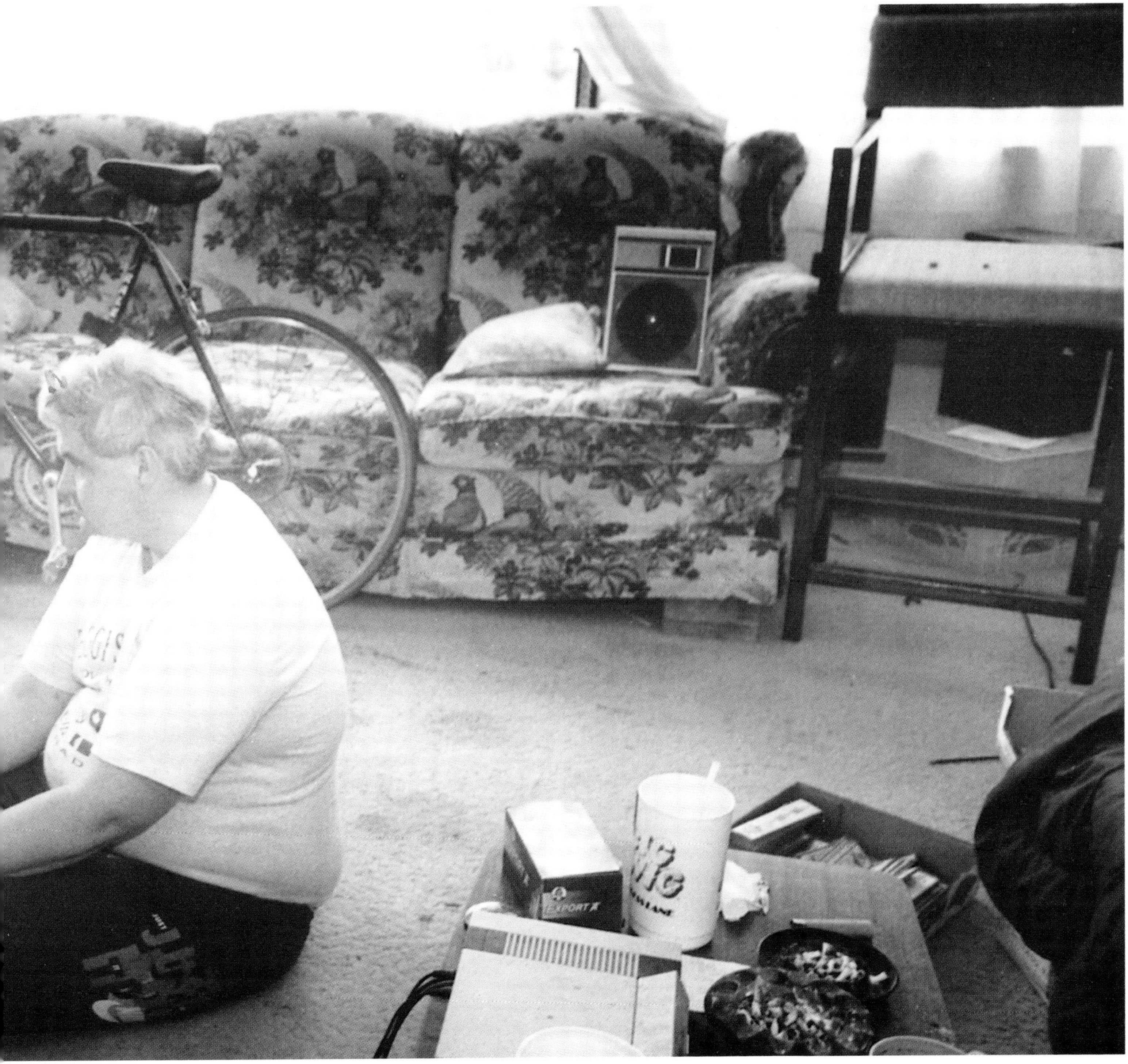

So who do you get to talk to about all of this?
Sometimes to her, sometimes my sister-in-law.

What does your family think about you getting married?
They aren't happy. They have to get to know Maxine really good. . . . My Mom's in the hospital for the seventh time now.

You've said your Mom didn't really like Maxine. How have you dealt with that?
I back Maxine up and I told my Mom, 'No more of this'. I have to re-zone you. I don't want to talk to you, I don't want to phone you anymore. I don't want you in my life any more.

That must have been a really hard step to take.
Yeah. And Maxine knows I back her up all the way.

Does Maxine back you up all the way?
Sometimes. . . .

But you feel that sometimes she doesn't totally back you up?
No.

How does that feel?
It feels good.

So that's okay? You understand?
Yeah. I want to be with her all times. Like I went to the swim meet on Sunday—and she . . . asked Wade to come. That was one bad mistake. He got me really upset. I walked outside and kicked one of the barrels, a big drum like they haul diesel in . . . I kicked that and it went airborne—that's how angry I was.

How did you deal with being angry after you kicked the drum?
I felt good. . . . One of our coaches calmed me down. . . . I told [Maxine] what did you bring *him* for? I was trying to concentrate on our swim meet. . . . Of course, I won two seconds and a third. And Maxine won a first, and two seconds, and two thirds.

Al calls himself a 'crazy collector' of unusual objects such as bus tokens and pop tops. An extensive collection of hats line the walls of his bedroom. His favorite features a Canadian beaver on the top, complete with ears and tail.

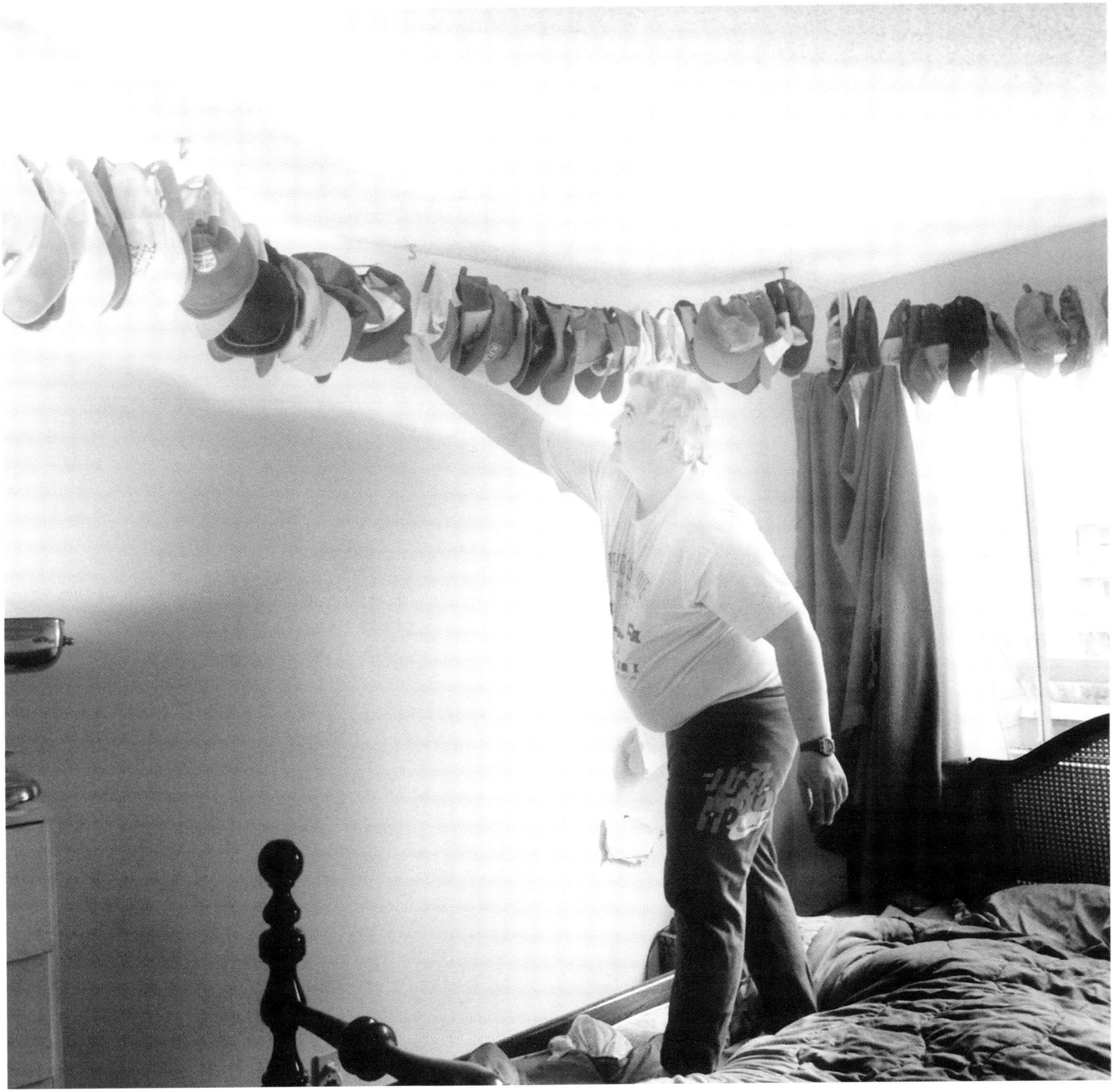

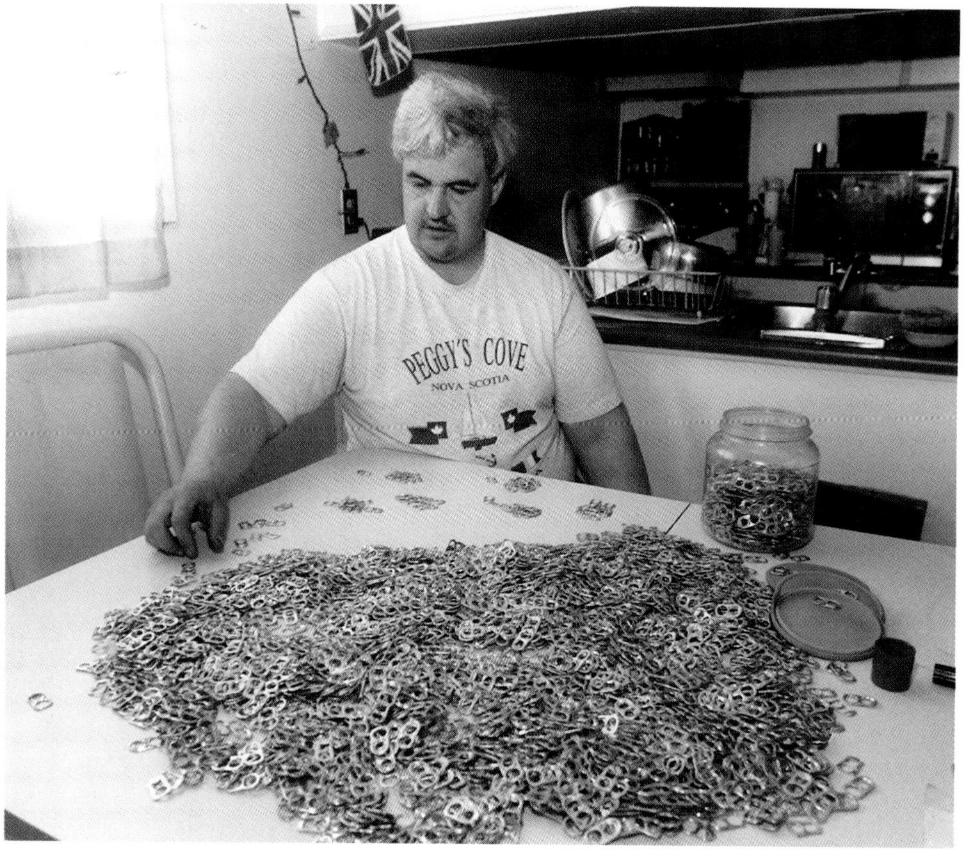

Tobacco tins and jars brimming with pop tops fill Al's kitchen. He estimates he has over 10,000 and delights in counting them out in groups of 10. He is collecting them in support of a charity for children with disabilites

Facing page: A maintenance job in his apartment complex helps Al meet the monthly rent.

Sports are a real interest that you and Maxine share. Are there other interests you share?
Sometimes her and I go for walks.

Are most people supportive of your relationship?
Yes. My friends who really care, don't want us to break up. . . . We have good times together.

And that's what's important for you?
Yeah.

AL'S WRITING

AL AND MAXINE MACLEOD

I met Maxine on the bus. She was with her fiance and I was with my girlfriend. She kept looking at me. I met her again at the Summer Games. On July 10, at a dance for the special Olympics' I asked her to dance. She told me she broke up with her fiance and I asked her if she wanted to go out with me. On our first date we went out for supper and went to meet her sister. She liked me.

We like to do things together. We go out for dinner and to movies. I see her at swimming and bowling. Now Maxine is learning to do more things without me but she still loves me. It will work out with her. We will be together. I love her. I asked Maxine to marry me on her birthday, in front of the swimming team. I felt happy because she said "yes." When we told Maxine's family they were shocked. For two years everything was okay until her brother stepped in. Now we are not engaged. Wade, a man from Maxine's group home took my girl. I do my thinking while walking and collecting beer bottles. My walks calm me down. I am not angry anymore. I am taking it one day at a time. I am still seeing Maxine but we are taking things slowly. I hope we can work it out.

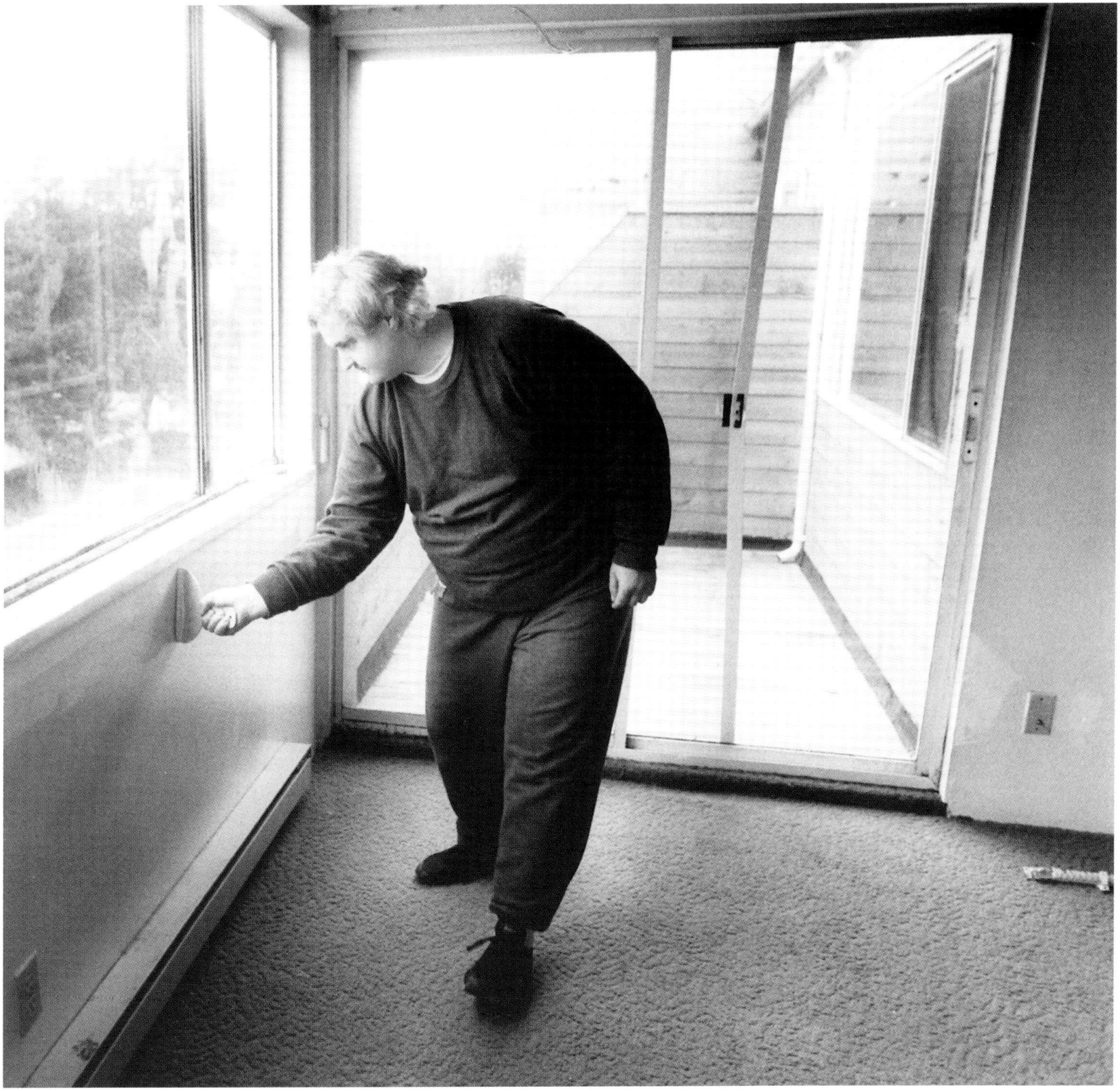

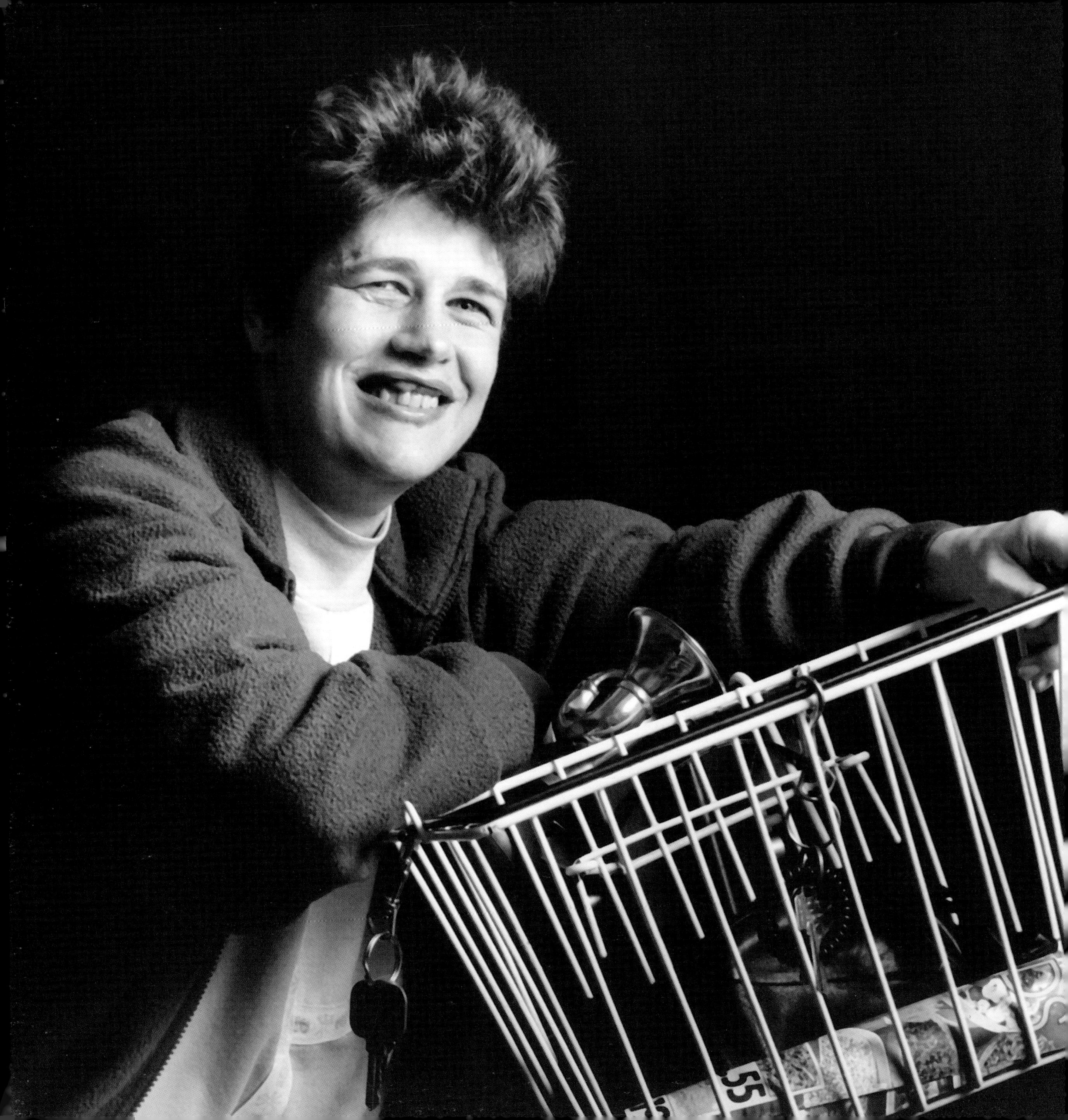

JANICE STEVENSON

Defining herself as an activist and a fighter, Janice (36) says most of her energy these days goes into coping with getting what she needs. She's waiting for a leg brace that will keep her knee in place and help prevent her from falling.

Janice has cerebral palsy and epilepsy. She has lived on her own for six years. Before she moved into her own place she lived in a life skills home for three years where she learned how to cook and clean, and what foods to eat to keep herself healthy. Janice says her family isn't happy she lives on her own, and she has chosen to have very little contact with her parents in order to preserve her independence.

She has held jobs working in restaurants and looking after children; but she is frustrated that it is so hard for people with disabilities to get good paying jobs. Several years ago, she won a case against an employer who didn't pay her fair wages.

Janice has several good friends she spends time with, but her passion and drive is in fighting for the rights of people with disabilities, by standing up for herself.

JANICE'S STORY

You wanted to talk about a struggle you went through recently.
Yes. It's really hard to get what you need. My scooter was hard to get. I had to fight the Welfare office for it. They said I couldn't use it because I have epileptic seizures. I had to go to a person that's farther up top, to be able to get my scooter, had to go visiting him in Vancouver. I had to take a bus to go down to Vancouver. It was a tough struggle because at that time I'd split my helmet in half. I had to be careful. Helmets are fifty dollars each. Welfare's skinny on that too. They don't want to give wheelchairs or scooters or whatever. It's frustrating.

How did you convince them?
I had to go to the top person, in Vancouver, to talk to them. "Do you want me to split my head open and fall down and have bruises on my face and whatnot, to be in the hospital every six weeks, from the falling down? Which would you rather pay? Would you rather pay for the damages or would you want to help me live?"

So you were telling them it was safer and cheaper for you to have a scooter than for you to have to keep going to the hospital. Did you do this by yourself?
Yes I did. It was harder and harder and harder each day that I had to go downtown. Each day was different. I'd make appointments, and went down there at the time I was supposed to be down there. Sometimes I got a ride, sometimes I didn't. Sometimes I had to take the bus. It would depend on how well I was or if I was sick. I was pretty ill at that time. I had to deal with other things as well besides the Welfare office. It was like I couldn't cope with it. Every day was different. It was frustrating.

How did you get through it?
Well . . . with the difficulty [of falling], of kissing the floor, kissing the pavement, each day was different. Each time [it happened] I had to get my pictures taken. Each time I took a picture into the Welfare office. They just ripped it up. They didn't want to see what my face looked like; they didn't want to see what my body was like. They didn't care. Well, I took those pictures; I had negatives. I decided well okay, this is not working, because Welfare will not do anything. So I'll go to the higher-up because

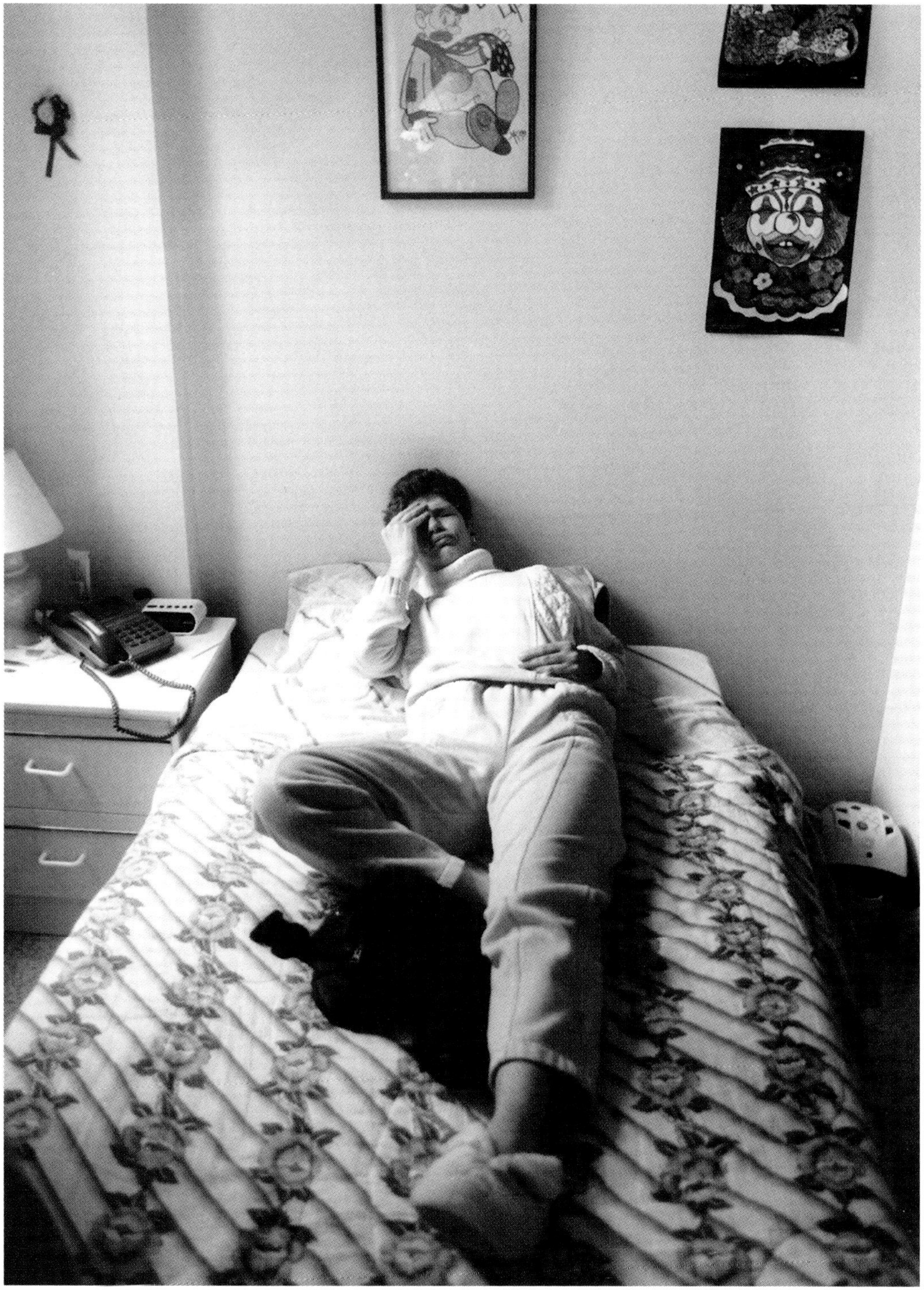

When a long-awaited wheelchair didn't fit, Janice endured delays and endless phone calls trying to get it replaced. The experience left her frustrated and exhausted.

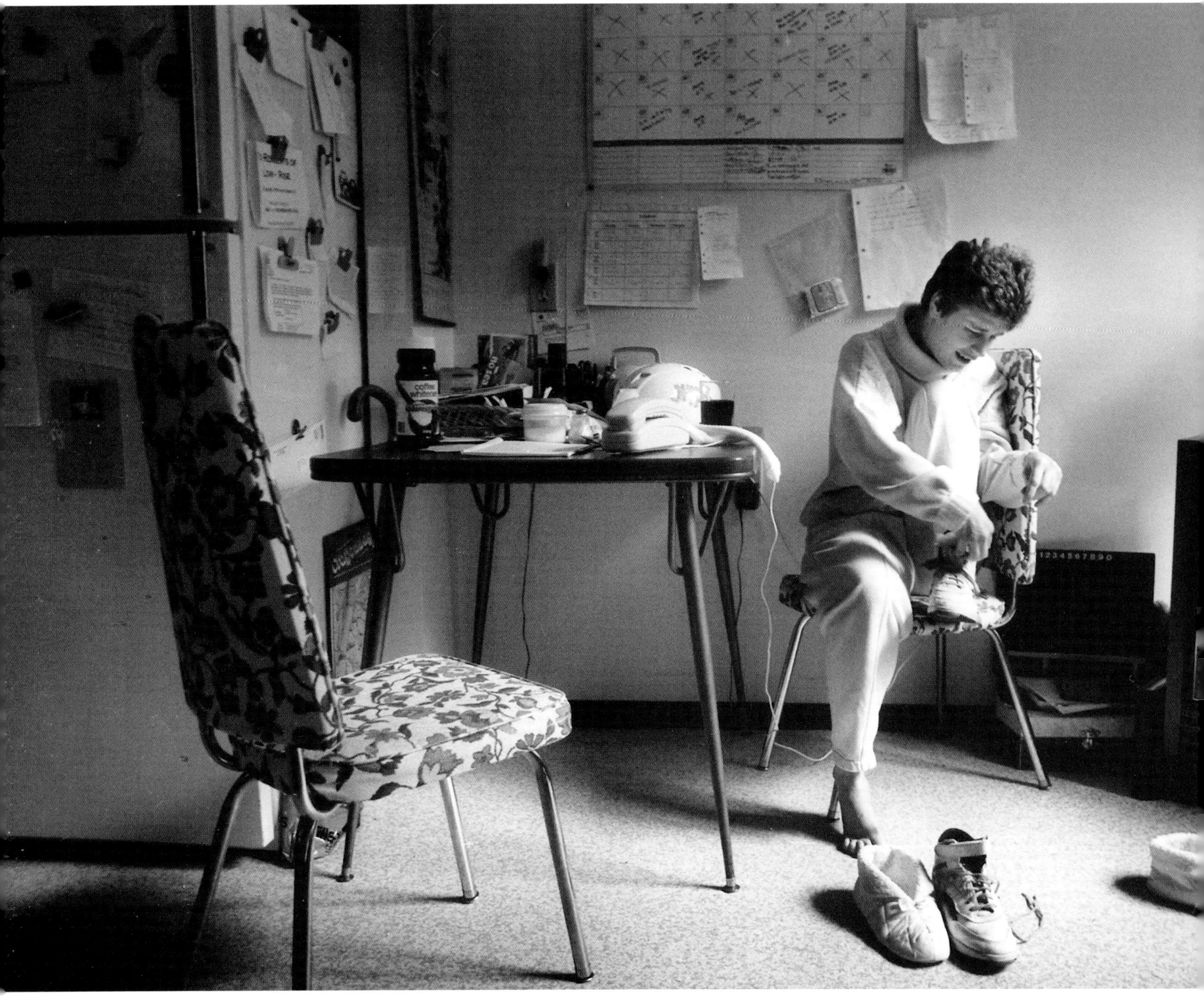

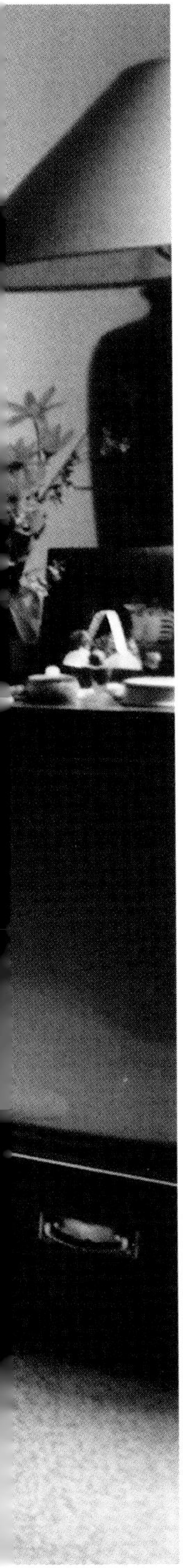

this is not going to work. I'm not getting my scooter and I'm going to be kissing the floor more if I keep this up.

To add to that it was like, okay, the guy I was talking to said, "You've got every right to fight for what you want. It's not going to do you any good if you keep kissing the floor. You'll break your nose or whatever." I said, yeah, I know. Every six months I have to get a new helmet.

Who was this guy?
The higher guy [closer to the top official] I needed to speak with to be able to get the scooter and whatever else I needed. I'm still fighting with them because I need a new brace for my leg. They said no, you can't have that.

How long did it take to get the scooter?
Six and a half weeks of going down there . . . back and forth . . . downtown . . . up, down . . . kiss the floor . . . go outside in the snow. Eventually I managed to get what I wanted. But I'm still struggling for a few more things that I need. I need a hand brace, I need a new brace for my knee. They're trying to tell me I can't have that one because I don't deserve it. So I have to go back to the higher-up again, and fight again.

What reason do they give for you not deserving it?
Money is tight. I'm supposed to try and do it myself and to forget that it's not fair. I'm ready to explode because people are not listening to what I'm trying to tell them. I'm trying to get my own self together, so that I can do things. But they don't listen to me.

So I have to fight—with some help—because if I don't get what I need, I'm going to go back to the hospital. What I'm dealing with now, I'm falling down in my own apartment. I should have railings around my apartment so I wouldn't fall down when I walk around the house. But Welfare will not pay for those things.

I've struggled to get what I need because if I don't, I might as well say good-bye.

Janice gets ready for an afternoon of shopping. She delights in her independence & is able to go most places without assistance.

Page 48: Aware of how strongly her life is affected by provincial health and welfare policies, Janice casts her vote in a provincial election.

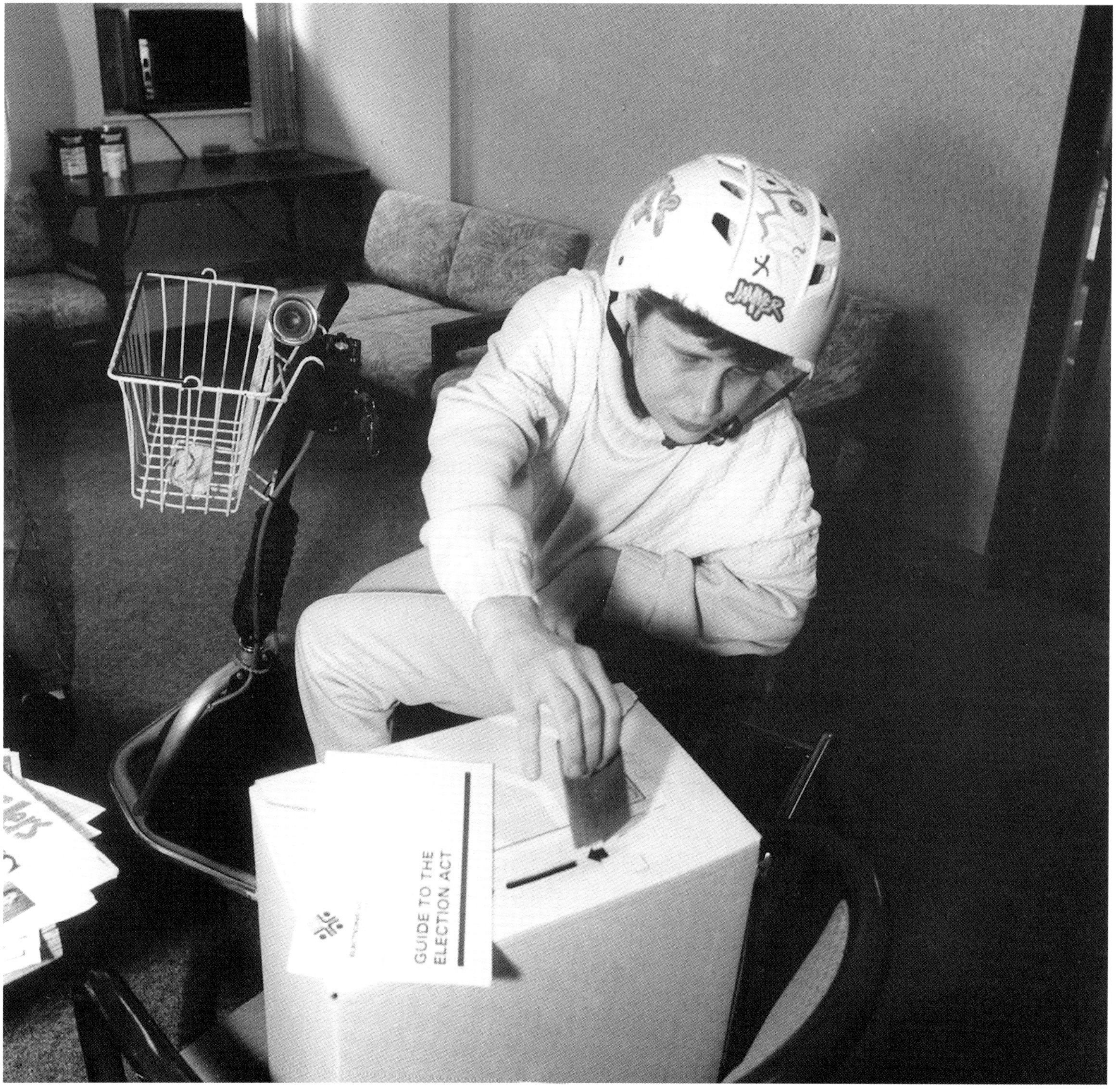
GUIDE TO THE
ELECTION ACT

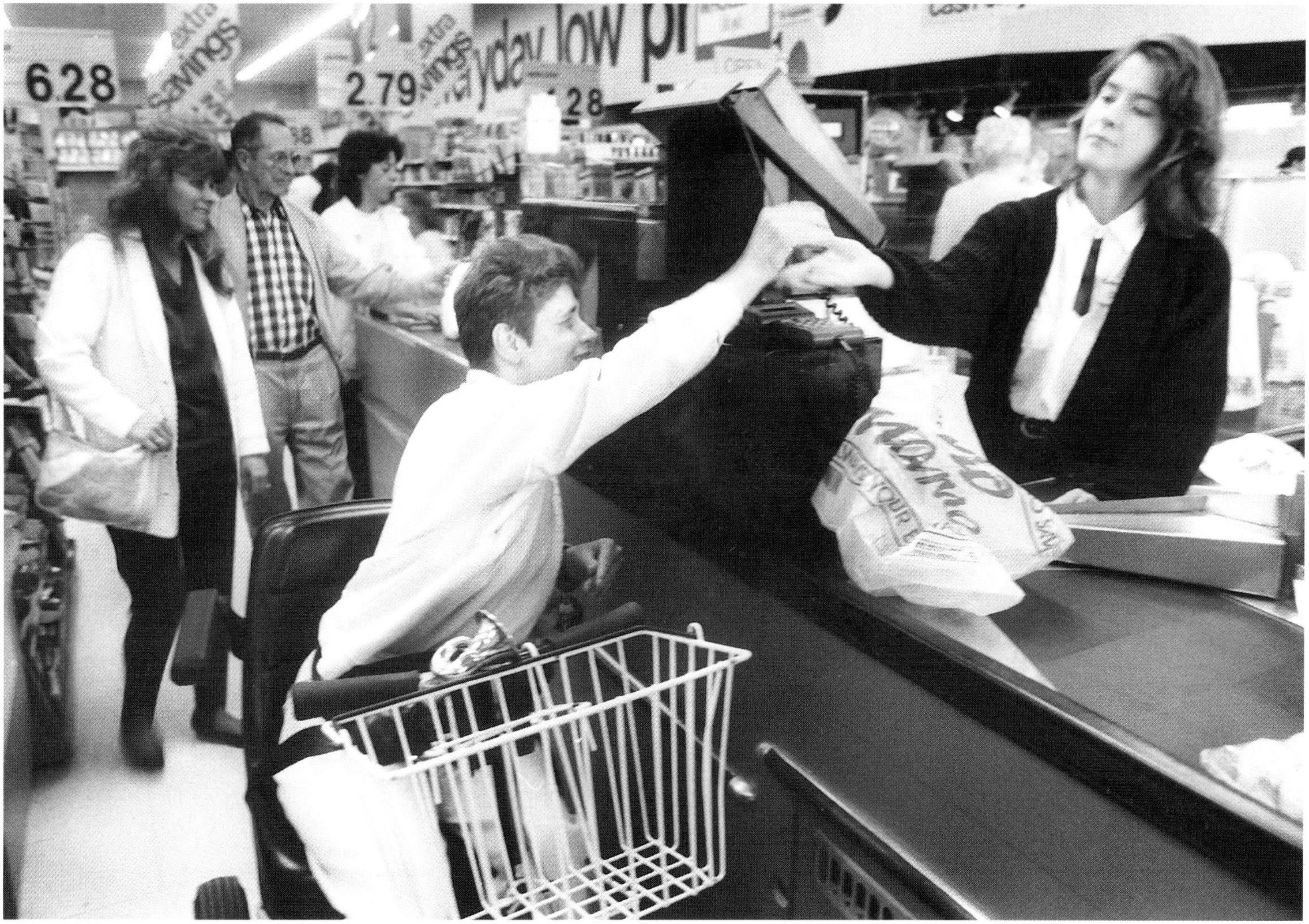

What's given you such determination to keep on fighting?
I've got people who are trying to help me do it. That's what's keeping me together. But at the same time, they don't want to see me hurt. If I hurt myself any more, they're going to see me in a morgue.

It's not fair. You've got to fight for what you believe in. But somehow it doesn't work, and I'm frustrated with that, because it's not working out too well. I'm trying to figure out what to do with the rest of my life.

A court case is coming up that I've got to deal with, with my family and stuff.

After a long fight, Janice received a motorized scooter which serves as her primary means of transportation. She rides it to school and to the local shopping mall where she buys groceries, window shops and enjoys coffee in a cafe.

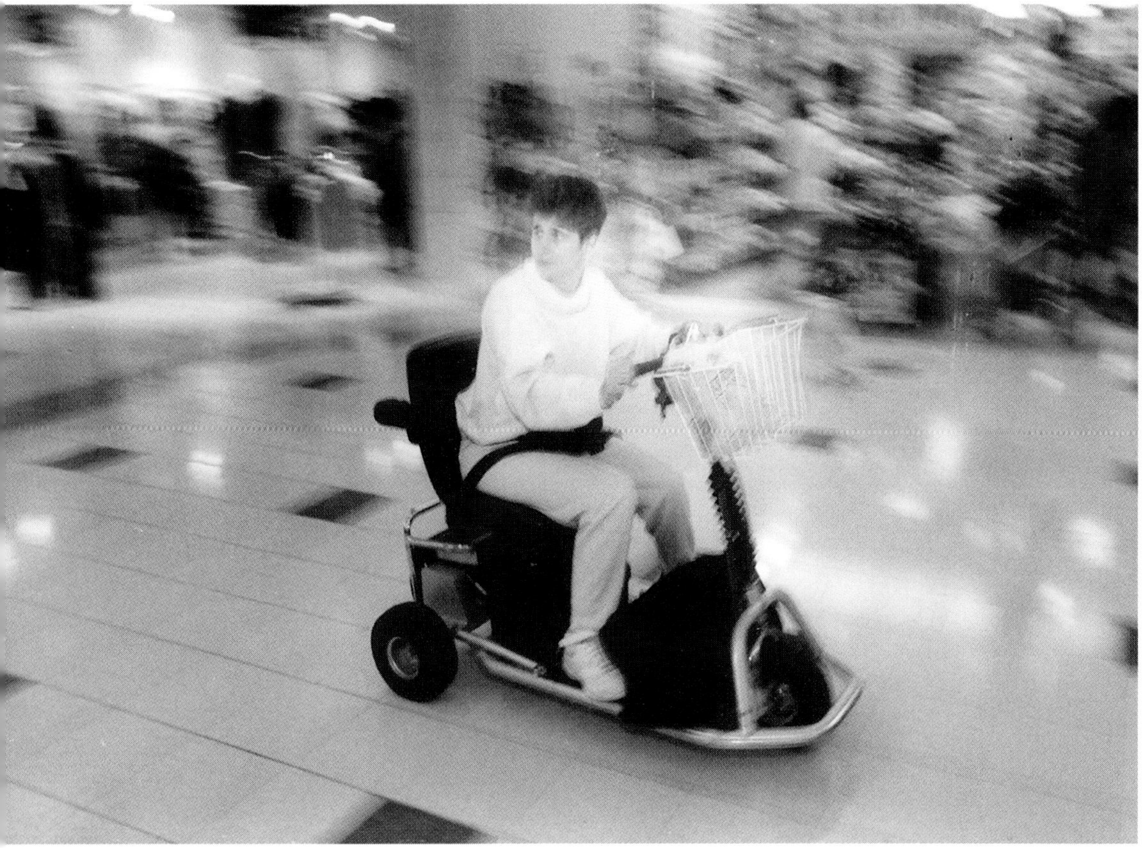

That's coming up pretty quick. My family has decided not to have anything to do with me because I [have a] disability. They think that I'm no good, so I'm starting to believe all of that.

What are you going to court for?
Because they think that I'm uncapable to take good care of myself.

Your family is trying to have you declared . . .
Uncapable.

So you're going to court to fight that?
Yes.

That must be really awful.
Yes. It is tough to realize that my family has decided that. I have to go to court after Christmas. [And] right after Christmas I have to go to the hospital to have some more tests done. They think that I'm uncapable. I have been told that I have to do all these tests to prove that I can be on my own. I'm living on my own right now, while we speak. It's just not fair that I have to fight with everybody in this world to get what I need. You know, it's frustrating to have to deal with people [in accordance with the] Disabilities Act. Yet. . . .

How long have you been living on your own?
Now it's been about three years, I'd say. Roughly.

You've been doing it that long, but your family has now decided . . .
. . . decided to interfere. I have to keep going till I can get what I need. I need some stuff so I can get to what I want to do and be happy. But I'm not going to get that way if people don't help me to get what I want.

JANICE'S WRITING

MY SCOOTER

It was very challenging to try to talk to Welfare about my wanting a scooter. I wanted a scooter because I kiss the floor too many times—falling on my face. Each time I fell I always hurt different parts.

I asked for a scooter three years ago. I have C.P. which makes me lose my balance . . . my legs kind of cave in. At first I asked my worker and she said no. I do a lot of things I need the scooter for. I go shopping, go to the bank, and go to school to learn to read and write.

I then went higher, above my worker. I went to speak to a man who fights for people who have disabilities and need someone to speak for them. He helped me fight Welfare for it. I went to his office every day to fight. I had to write a letter about the reason I needed a scooter. This fight took me three years and I finally got my scooter. Right now I'm trying to fight for something else—my independence.

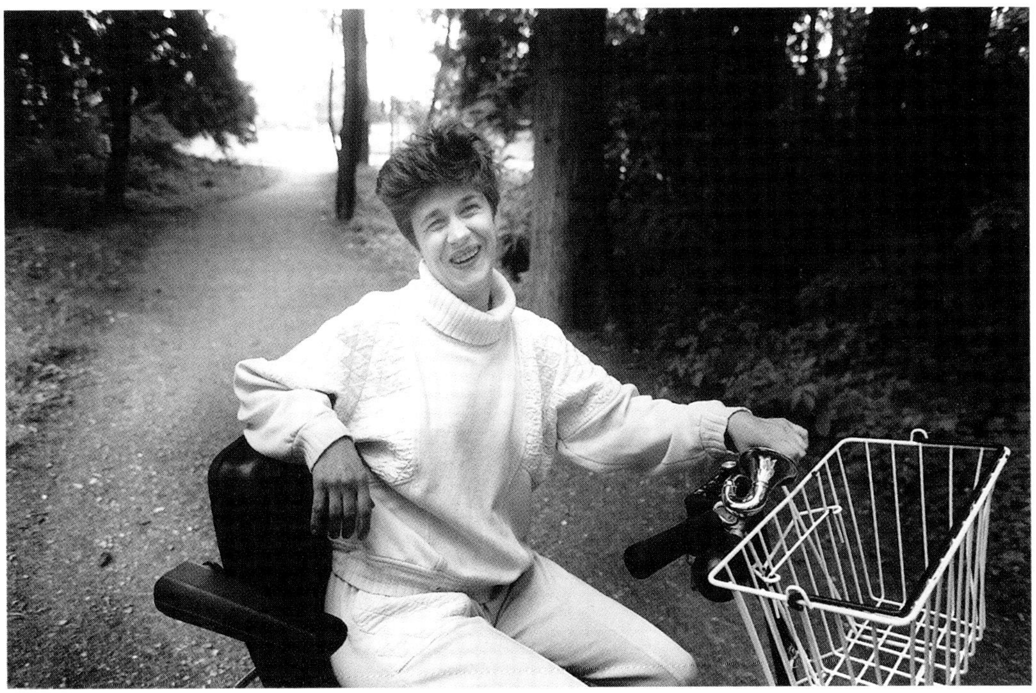

Despite her battles still ahead, Janice savours the victories won by her relentless crusading.

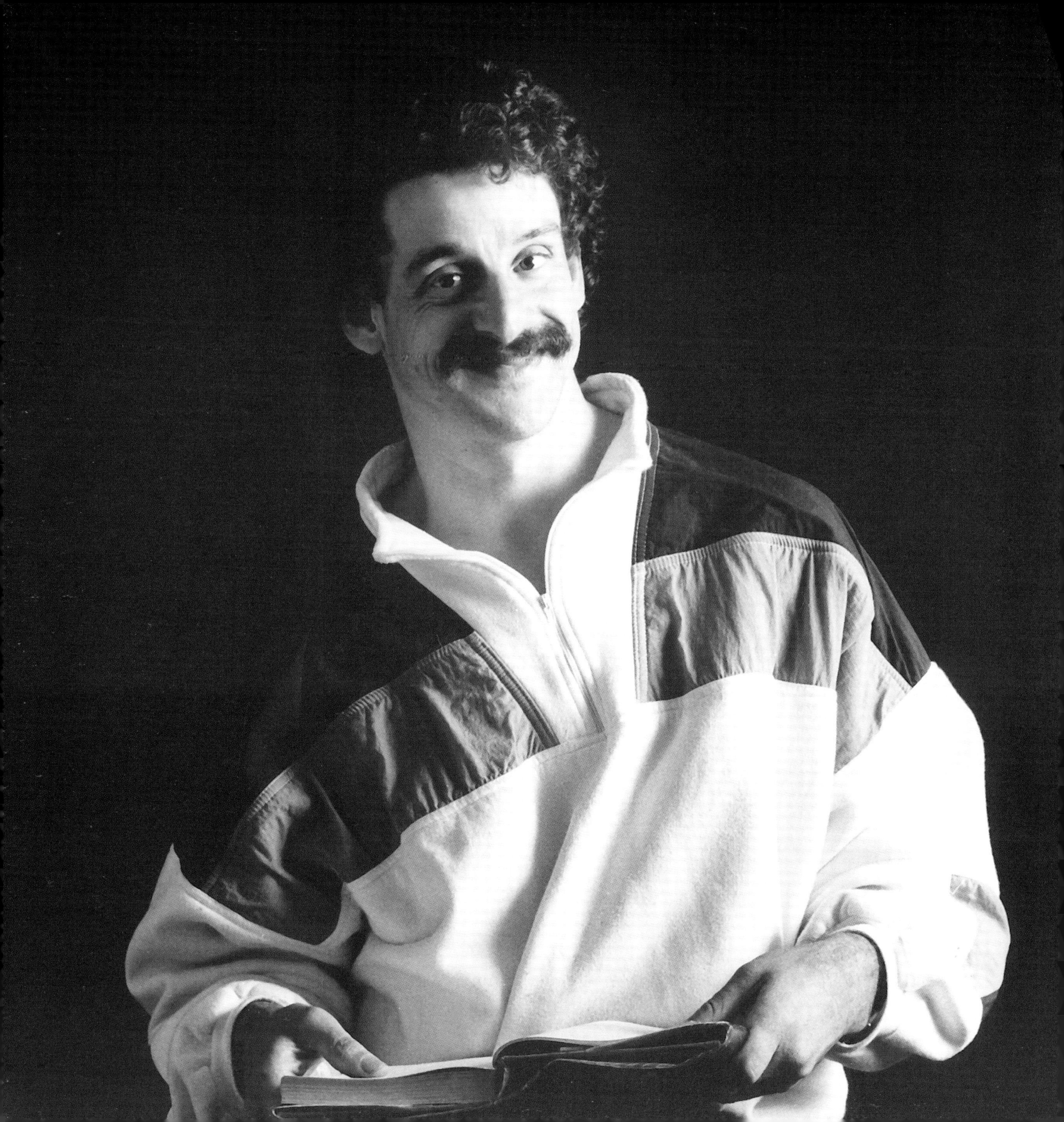

TONY LOUREIRO

Tony (36) is known for his ability to remember birthdays. He says that if anyone tells him a birthday, he keeps it in his head. Around the Invergarry Learning Centre he's recognized for his thoughtfulness in getting birthday cards for teachers and other staff. Tony has been attending Invergarry full time for several years, but recently decided to come only one day a week.

Besides attending Invergarry, Tony volunteers at the SPCA. He works every Saturday. His job is helping people decide which dog will be the best one for them to adopt. He really likes finding good homes for the stray dogs.

Tony spends much of his time alone, in his own apartment. He does lots of writing at home. Every summer he goes back to Oliver, B.C. to stay with his parents and look after his cousin's orchard. He's very close to his parents. His parents speak Portuguese, and Tony says he understands it better than he speaks it, even though it is his first language.

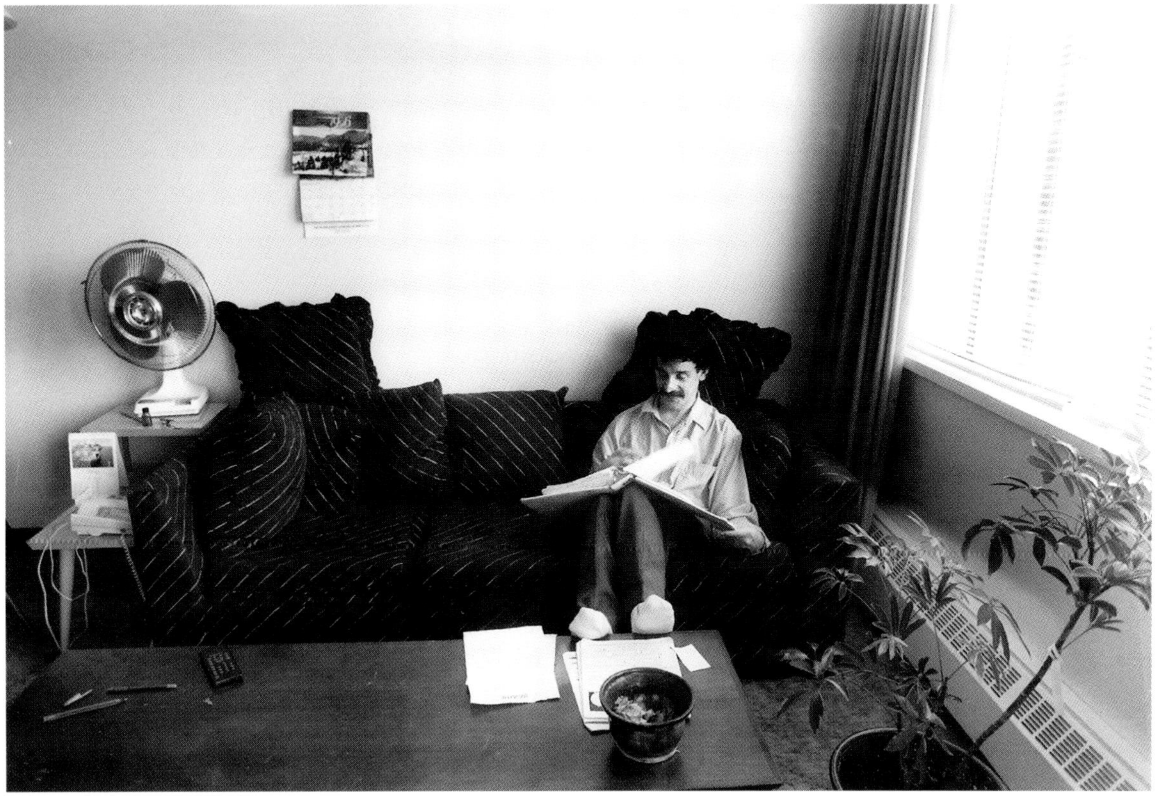

TONY'S STORY

Let's begin with the accident.
I was walking along on the sidewalk and this car hit me. And the man in the car which hit me said, 'Sorry sir, I was trying not to get hit by a truck.' Myself, if I was a driver I would prefer to get rear ended by a truck than hit someone on a sidewalk. I said, 'Okay, lets call the police.' So we called the RCMP and he got on the phone and said I tried to jump his car. There's no way I could jump his car. There's no way.

He gave me a piece of paper with his name and his license number, then he left. He left the scene. And that's where it was left. Then a year later, he beat a traffic ticket. It was during the spring break and I was at my family doctor in Vancouver because of the accident.

So he beat a traffic ticket that he got from the accident where he hit you?
Then he tried to sue me a year later because I didn't show up for a traffic ticket. But by law you cannot sue anybody for a traffic ticket because they don't show up. Then I went to Supreme Court and I passed it. Now it was supposed to go to Supreme Court in February but it's over with because it was settled before that in January.

So you had an out-of-court settlement?
Yes. And the Insurance Corporation of British Columbia agreed that if he comes after me again ICBC will take care of it.

What are you going to do now?
I'd like to get a computer cause it's easier to work.

Preferring the privacy of his apartment for studying, Tony takes great pride in his large potted plants, coordinated furniture and meticulously organized closet.

What kind of work?
Like for spelling and things like that. For writing and games. But I don't really care for games.

Why is writing important to you?
So I don't have to depend on other people to read my private letters. If I have to get someone to read it, it won't be private anymore.

Why is privacy so important for you?
If I get a friend to read it, it won't be private anymore. One minute you can get a friend to read it for you, and then the next it's not a friend. It's not private anymore.

So you fear that if people are reading your stuff they're going to find out things that will make them not want to be your friend?
Sometimes.

Has that happened?
No, not so far. If it turns out it's really important and no one is supposed to know but myself, it's not private anymore. And that's one of the reasons why I want to get a computer and type it in and then the computer will read it to me.

You want to have a talking computer. Have you ever worked with a talking computer?
Yes. SARAW it's called.

Anything else you want to say?
If anyone has an accident, if anyone hits them make sure they go and see a lawyer. And every disabled person has rights as well as everybody else. I didn't really care how much I was going to get.

The money wasn't important, it was the idea of standing up for your rights?
The idea was more to get your rights.

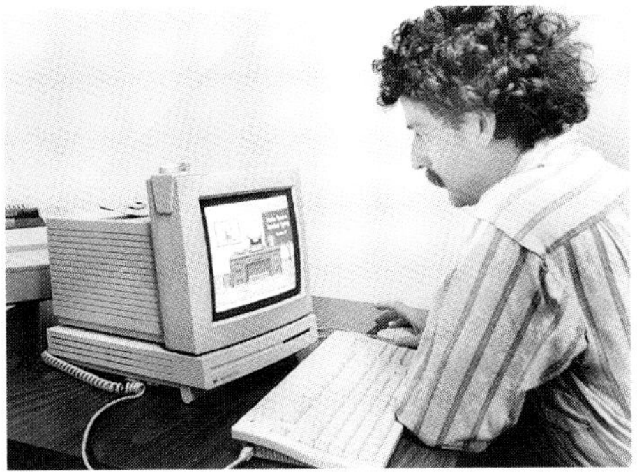

Tony explores a computer at Invergarry Learning Centre.

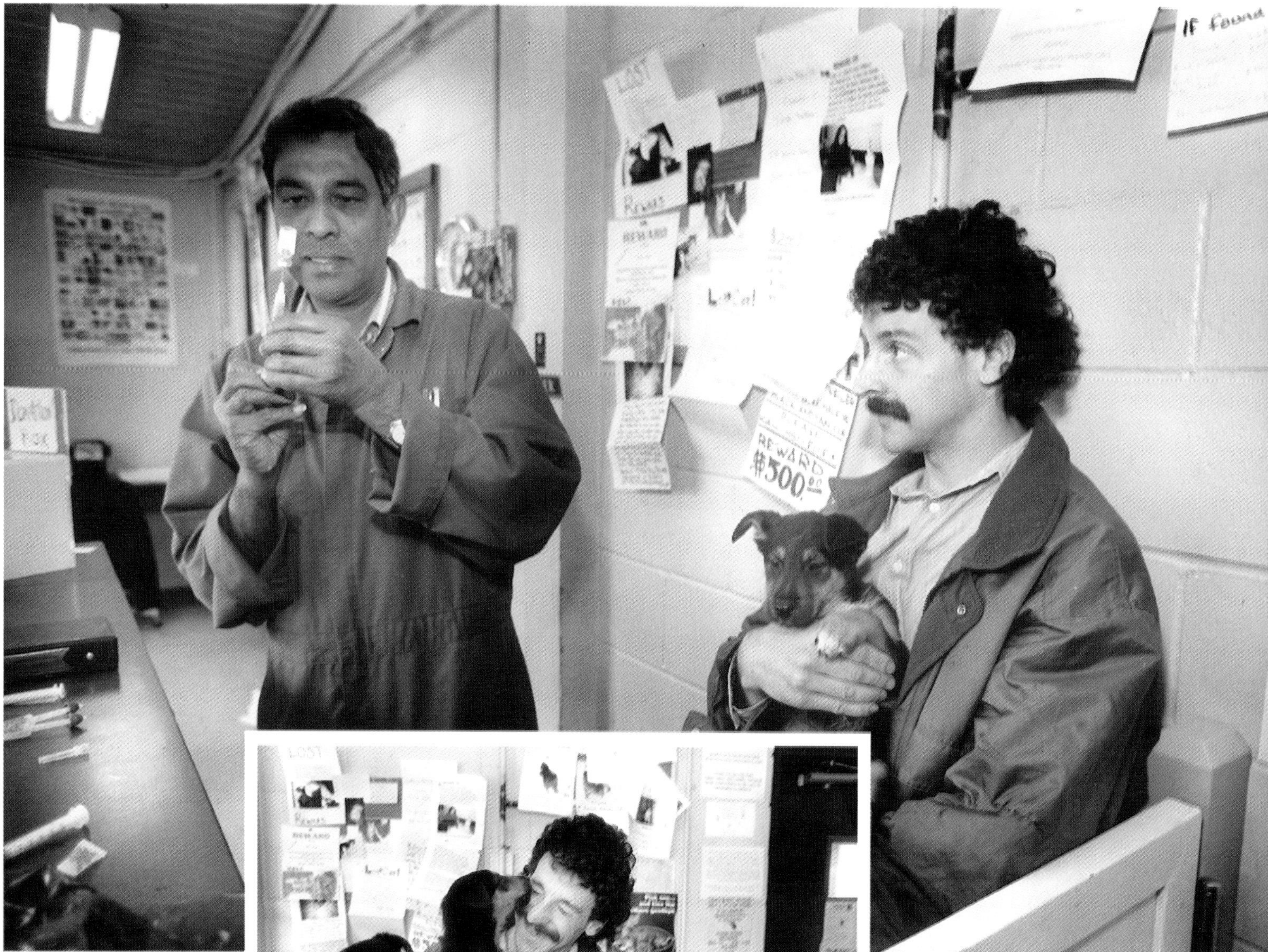
LOST
REWARD

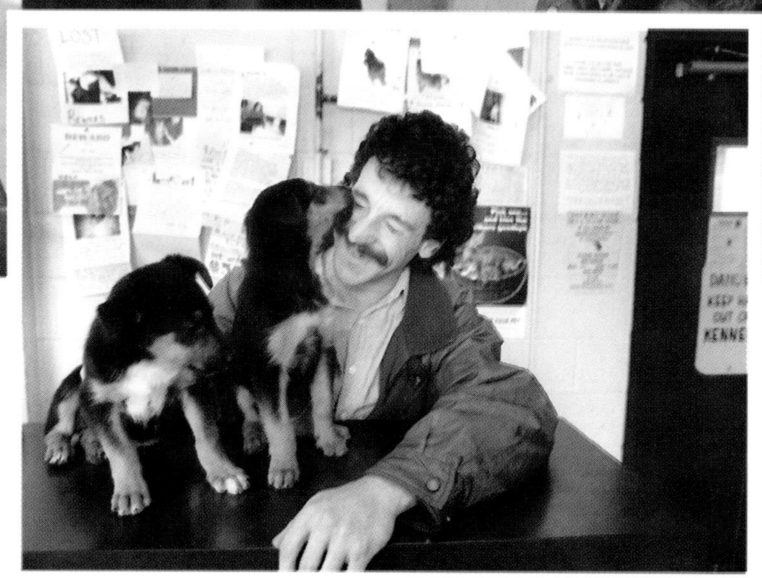

TONY'S WRITING

TONY—MY STORY

I was born on March 5th, 1960 in Oliver, B.C. I weighed 6 lbs. 6 oz. I had a real tough start. When I was born I was supposed to be six feet under (dead). There were problems with my legs. I got corrective surgery on my legs when I was two or three. Then I had to wear leg braces and learn how to walk. It wasn't easy especially when I fell down, I had a hard time getting up. I wore the leg braces until 1969. I was nine years old then, I had to learn to walk without braces. Until I was about six or seven, I lived six months a year in the hospital and the other six months at home. Everytime I came home from the hospital I forgot how to speak Portuguese. It is the only language my parents speak at home.

I started going to school when I was five or six years old. First, I went to a school for disabled people called Fairview School. Then my parents argued with the school system and got me put in the regular school system. When I was 12 I got put back into Fairview School again until the age of 18. The schoolboard made this decision. Neither my parents nor I had any choice.

I worked in a small town called Oliver where people gave me a chance to work for them. I cut their grass, looked after their yard when they were away, watered their house plants and got their mail. They gave different amounts of money, depending on what their heart desired, for my pay. Then I went to regular high school to try and get reading and writing skills when I was 24. They had me doing errands instead, such as bringing absentee slips to different teachers and getting the mail from the Post Office.

They gave me $15.00 a month for these errands. The classes I attended there were too advanced for me, so I didn't learn. When I was 24, I got my driver's license. I was tested orally and I passed the first time. At 27, I went to Victoria to Goodwill Enterprises. At Goodwill Enterprises I went to a workshop where I trained to be a janitor. I couldn't read labels very well so I never worked as a janitor. After that I tried to get into the READ Society. I went to the B.C. government to get the funding but they said, no. They would give me funding to learn how to use a computer but not how to read and write. They decided this after looking at my school files. They believed I couldn't learn how to read and write because of what the files said, so I went back to Oliver. While I was watching the Knowledge Network I saw some

Facing page: In his part-time job at the SPCA, Tony helps with pet adoptions and other chores, including assisting the veterinarian who administers vaccines to incoming puppies. After their shots, Tony comforts the puppies with hugs and kisses. "If I could, I would release every dog in this place," her says

information about literacy at Invergarry Learning Centre in Surrey. I moved to Surrey and started at Invergarry. There was no waiting list when I started, so I got in right away. The hardest thing was finding a place to live. I moved five times until I got into B.C. Housing. I have lived in my place now for almost four years.

THE CASE: A TOUGH WORLD

I was walking by a gas station when a car turned off into the driveway of the gas station and hit me. I went over the car's front hood. The driver of the vehicle involved came out of the car and said, "Sorry, sorry, I was going to get rear ended by a truck." I couldn't see any truck or any other vehicle involved. The driver was alone in his car; I was walking alone. There was traffic on the street, but no one stopped. The girl attendant at the gas station called 911 (Police) at my request. Even though I was the one who asked her to phone the police, she handed the phone to the car driver before it was handed to me. The driver spoke to someone on the phone and maintained that I tried to jump on his car. When the driver gave the receiver to me, I told the operator I didn't try to jump on his car, he is not telling the truth. When I spoke to the operator, I repeated what the driver told me. The 911 operator told me to stay with the driver until the police arrived. I asked the driver to stay until the police came but the driver left. The police attended for approximately 5 minutes and left me at the gas station. I walked home. My right leg was injured and scraped. My lower back was very sore the next day. I called a taxi. At the hospital I received a check-up and medication. The following day I experienced back pain and had to pay for another round trip by cab. I experience pain in my lower back, shoulders and stomach to this day, but during the first month following the incident I was unable to attend school because of severe discomfort.

The driver of the car got a traffic ticket, requiring him to pay $75.00 or dispute the traffic ticket in court. What I want to know is this: If my being in court was necessary to keep the case from being dropped, why didn't I get a subpoena or at least a notice in the mail? Because I was not there he was acquitted and he did not even have to pay the minimum $75.00 fine after running me down. I tried to reopen it, but I couldn't get it reopened. I tried writing letters but was told that a traffic ticket case can't be reopened.

The next thing I heard, the driver was trying to sue me. He was suing me to get his safe driver's discount back, for damages to his car, and for the time he had to take off of work. So, I got a lawyer. We went to Small Claims Court and the judge passed the case on to the Supreme Court. I had to go to "discovery" where they wanted to make sure I was telling the truth. After five hours of questions, I passed.

I may have a disability that is more noticeable than someone else's, but, everyone has a disability in some way. If you ever get into an accident call a lawyer right away, even if it's not your fault. If you get hurt you have to fight for your rights. Keep copies of everything, from the RCMP, insurance company and the lawyers, for yourself. If you have nothing to hide about your history give permission to the insurance company to look into it. This will make it much easier for you. Don't let anyone push you around. Stand up for your rights. Due to this accident I have a harder time trusting people. I like to keep things to myself.

I have a few close friends who I know I can trust. I enjoy doing things with them, such as going to movies, going out for dinner, talking, etc.

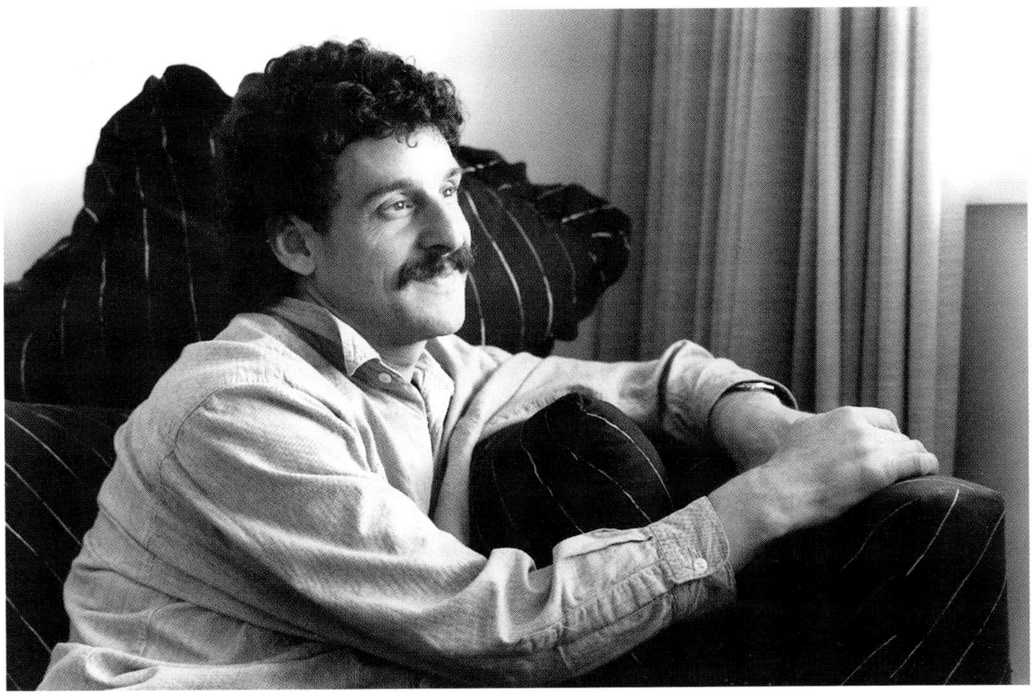

Tony dreams of one day using his improving reading skills to help others with literacy problems. "I think I would be good at it because I have been there myself," he says.

Page 60–61: It is uncomfortable for Tony to work in large groups. When he does attend classes, he prefers to work on an individual basis with his favourite and trusted teacher.

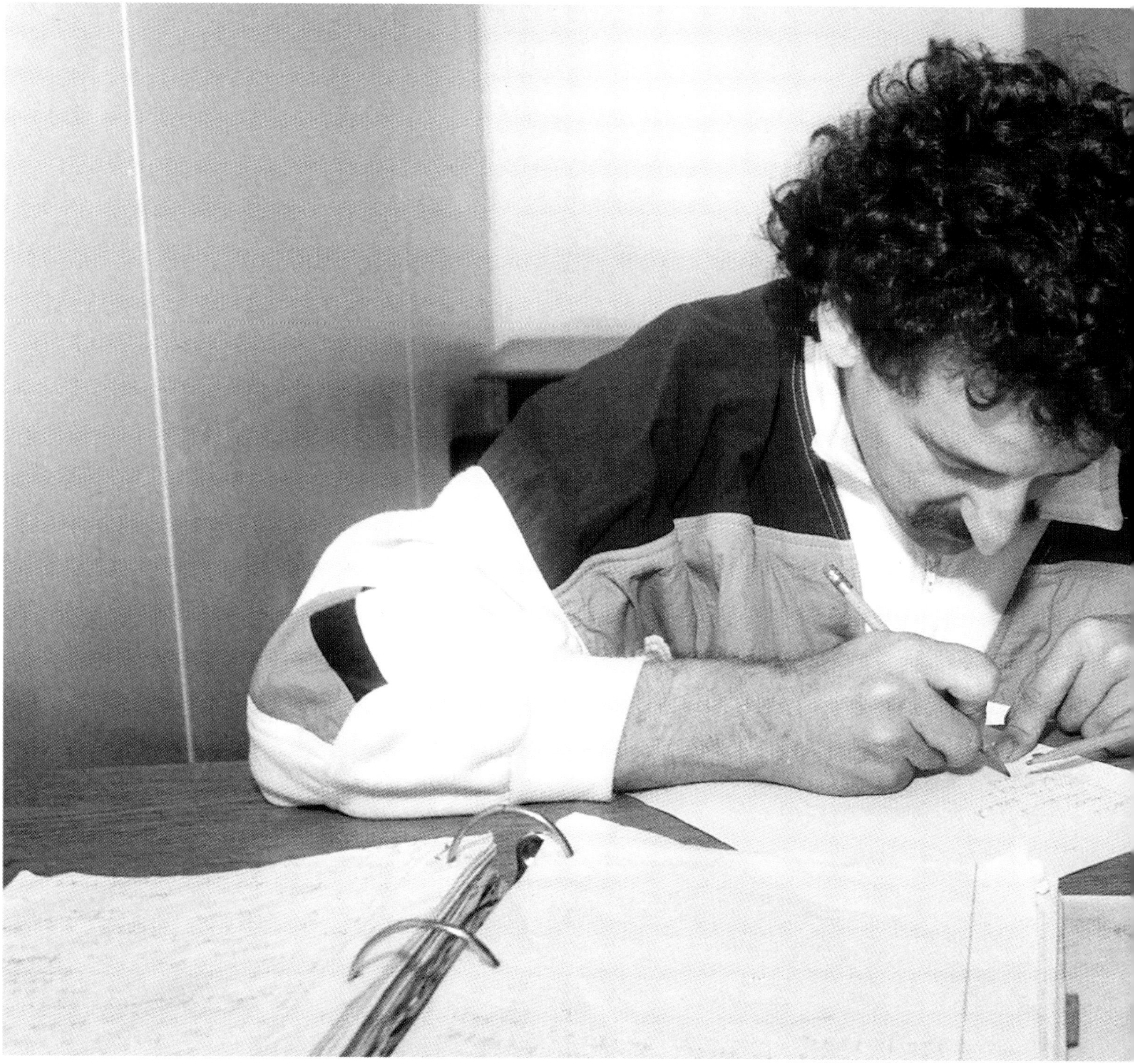

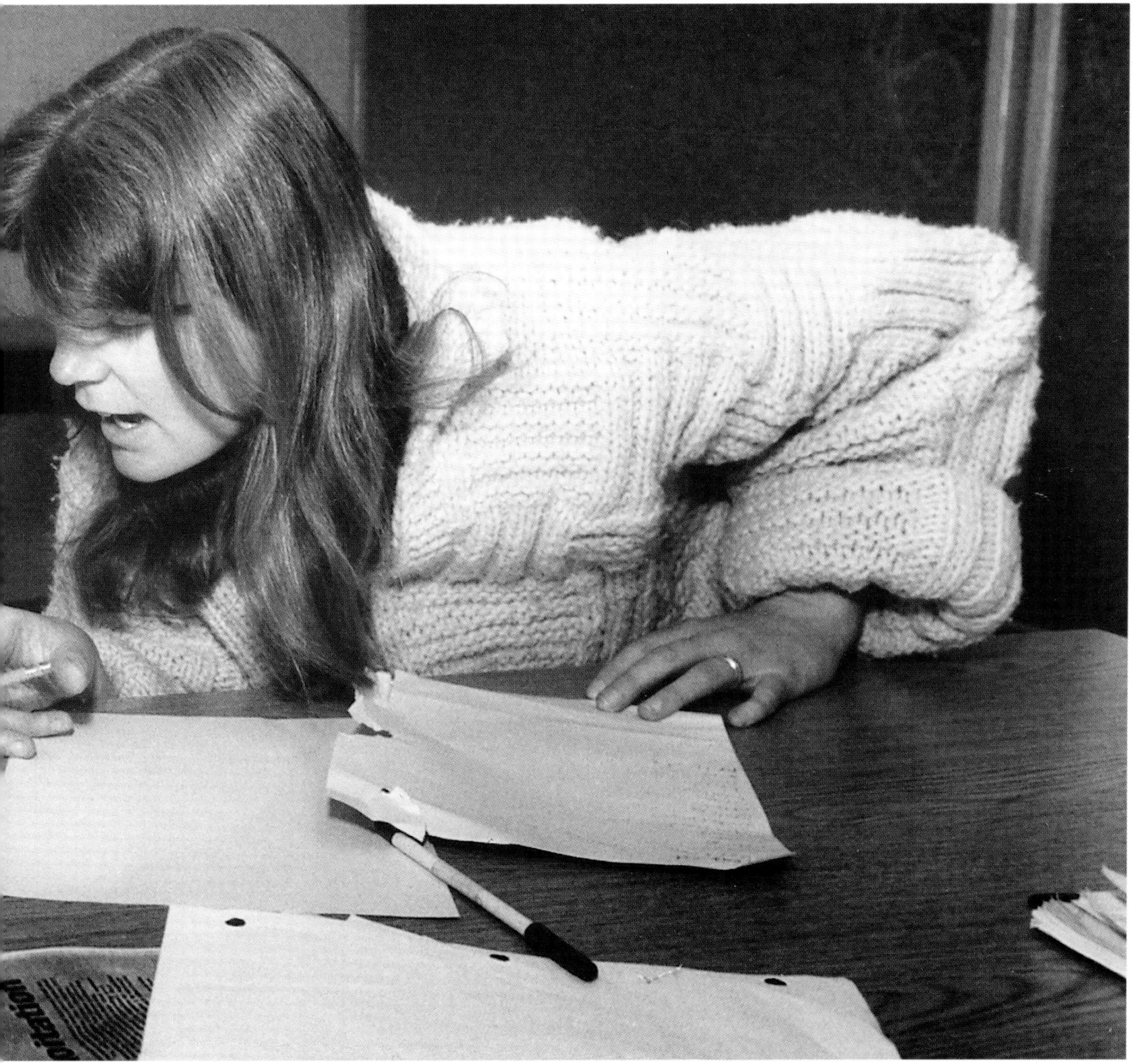

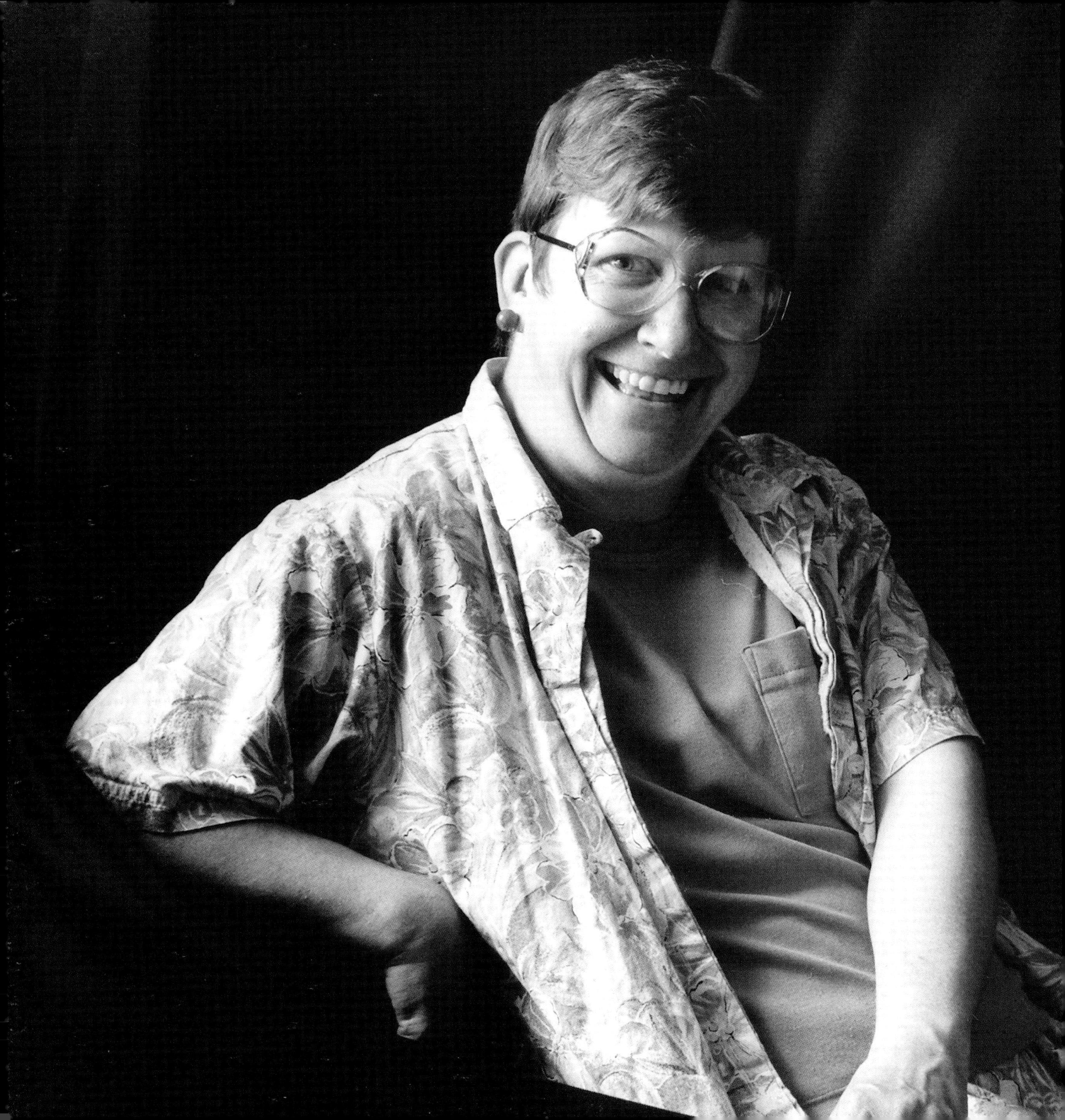

BARB GOODE

Barb (42) has been active in the self advocacy movement on behalf of people with mental disabilities for over twenty years. She has traveled to many parts of Canada and to other countries. In 1985, Barb was a part of a group of people that went to the highest court in Canada, the Supreme Court, to argue that people with mental disabilities should not be sterilized without their consent. They won the case.

Barb has also worked for several organizations that support self advocates. This included five years with the Rights Now project which went to three rural communities to teach people about self advocacy and to promote community living. Though she is less involved now with national and international work, she is still active with several groups in her own community. In particular, she loves helping people who are non-verbal find ways of expressing what they want in their lives.

Barb also loves to laugh and is very curious about the world around her. She reads, has a large collection of videos and a wide circle of friends. Currently unemployed, her time these days is spent seeking employment as a clerical worker, looking after her apartment, and keeping in touch with her large network of friends.

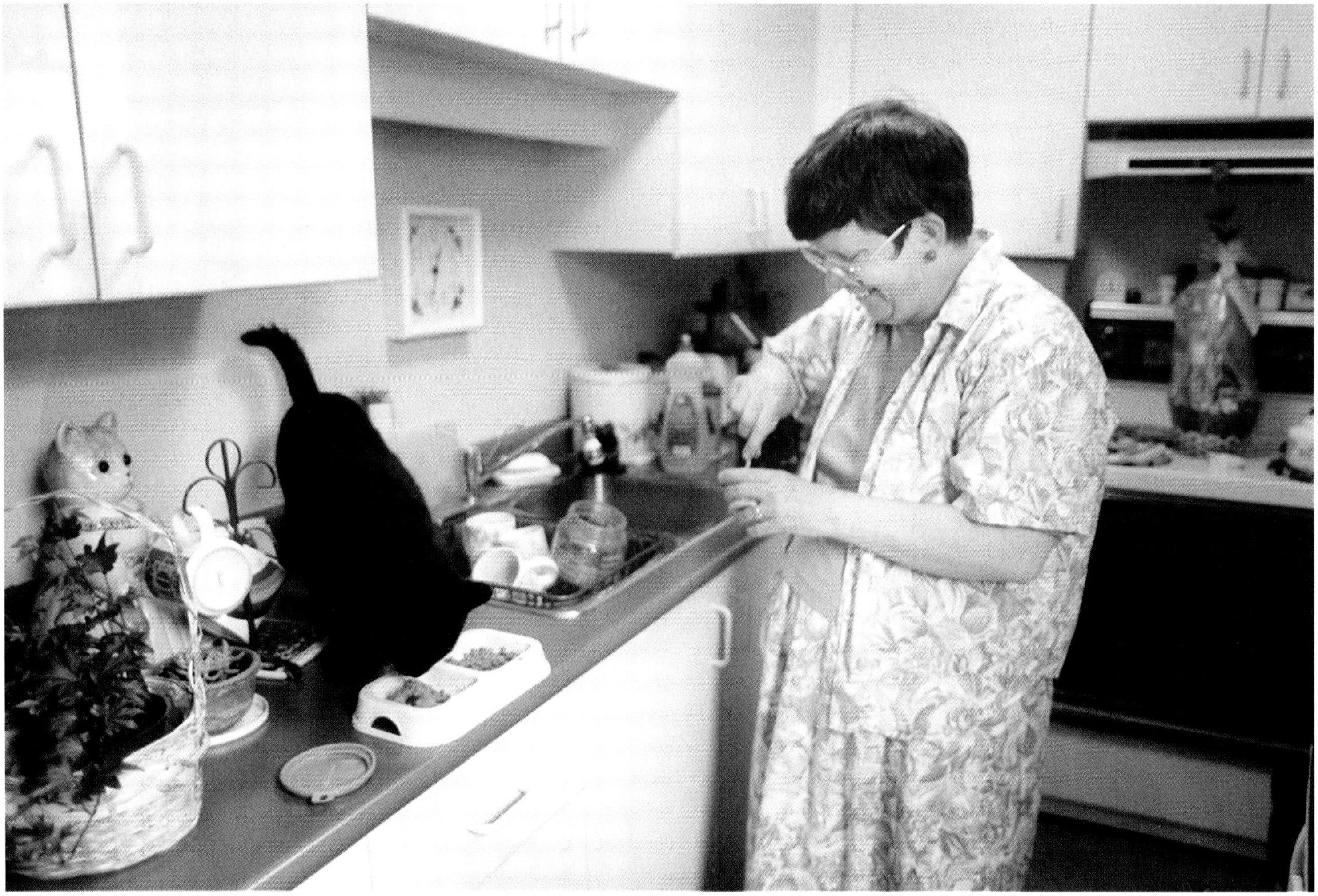

BARB'S STORY

Cuddles shares every aspect of Barb's life, including the kitchen counter for lunch.

You've said that this year you started thinking about getting a pet. How and why did you make your decision?
I was thinking that it would be good company. And a lot of people agreed with me. Then I finally decided myself without them persuading me. I thought go for it!

But I really didn't have a clue about how to look after something. So I had to learn how—get some information from different people. I thought it would be easier to get

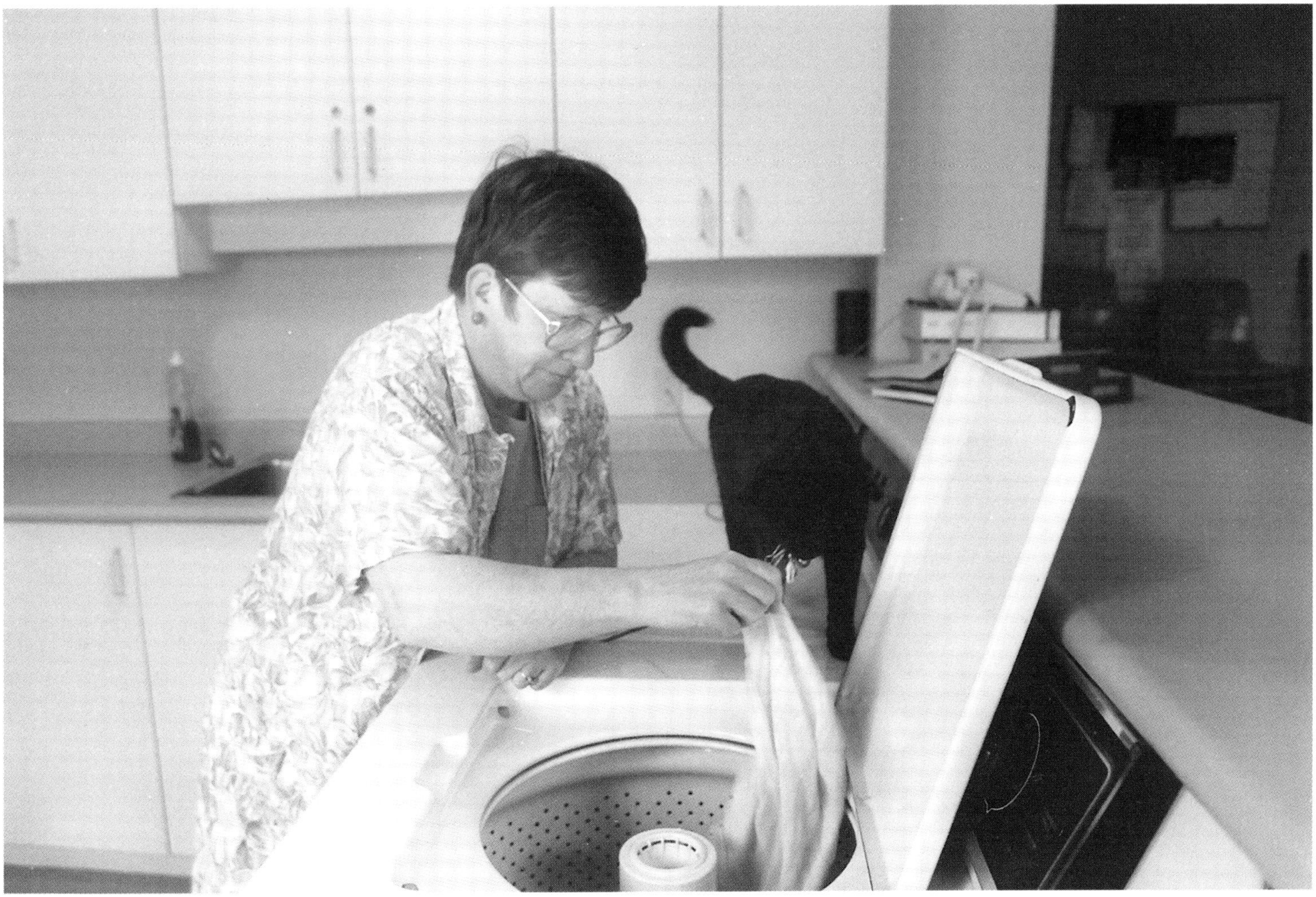

a cat than a dog. A dog is a lot harder to look after. In the daycare center next door they had a group of kitties, a litter, and they were getting rid of them.

"Cuddles loves to watch me do the laundry," Barb says. "If she goes missing, the laundry room is the first place I look."

Did you get your cat right away?
When I first heard about her, she wasn't old enough to leave her mother, so I had to wait awhile. Before I got her, I had to go and get a kitty litter and all the things

that I knew you had to have but I hadn't bought before. It was like shopping for a baby shower!

I brought her home when she was eight weeks old. I can remember. I picked her up and held her, and she was so scared she ran under someone's car and wouldn't come out. And when she finally came out, I brought her home.

Tell me about her name.

Cuddles. I always thought . . . I had thought for a long time that if ever I got a cat, I would want to have someone to cuddle with and snuggle with, and I always liked that name. I never told anyone for a long time what I was thinking. Sometimes I get very embarrassed when people ask me her name. Sometimes I just say CS or SC or whatever. But she really snuggles and we cuddle together, and it's kind of neat.

It still bothers me that people don't like her name, that they don't really understand why I call her that. But a name is a name. She knows her name.

Did you pick her out of all the other ones?

No. They asked me before I got her what color I wanted. They told me they had a black one, a white one, and a black-and-white one. I said, sure, a black one. They said she would grow out of being all black all over. But she's kept black so far.

People tried to tell me not to get a pet because they're a lot of money when you first get them. But I decided I wanted to have her.

And then when she was six months old—would it be six months old to get her spayed?—I had to decide if I should get it done or not.

I'm not for sterilization, which means not having babies, but I thought it's not a good idea to have kittens running around. I just felt like I wasn't doing her a favor by getting her to have babies at that age.

I can remember when she started menstruating, I just jumped the gun and thought it was something else. I thought something was wrong with her. Then someone told me she was menstruating and I thought, 'she's too young'. She wasn't even six months old then. As I said before, I didn't really understand cats. I never really had thought about an animal like her having babies. It just hadn't dawned on me that she could have babies if she wanted them.

You said you're against sterilization. What do you mean by that?

I'm not being funny . . . but what I mean is that when I was involved with a sterilization case of a human being, a woman, a group of us went to court saying, this woman shouldn't be sterilized without her consent. And I'm saying the same thing about Cuddles. She can't tell me if she wants babies or not—and it's the same with any animal. We decide if they should have kids or not. I don't know if that makes sense. To me it's just very important that she understands. But she doesn't understand.

I don't think I'd be a good mother. I'm not saying she wouldn't be, but I'm not sure I'm willing to let her try it. But [now] she can't have babies anyway.

So it's settled now. But it sounds like it was a complicated decision for you.
I wouldn't say complicated. But it wasn't easy. Part of me wanted to let her have babies and a part of me didn't. I just automatically thought back to the time when we took [the forced sterilization case] to the Supreme Court. . . . It's different, but in some ways it's not different. A lot of humans have [a number of] babies . . . and then they get sterilized. I wouldn't want *her* to have fourteen or fifteen babies that we couldn't sell or look after. So I guess it's the same kind of thing.

I can remember when I brought her home [after the operation] I thought I had killed her. She was so lifeless, she wouldn't do anything for almost three days. And I thought, 'Oh no. . . . What did I do. . . ?'

The other thing was, when I brought her home I was afraid. People kept scaring me, saying . . . she'll rip her stitches out. But she was quite calm about it. She was fine.

It sounds like Cuddles has made a lot of changes in your life.
I think she has. But some of them are hard. For one, being more responsible. If someone asks me to do something I think about it twice. I think about her, because instead of having to come home by myself and not worry about anyone but myself, now I have to worry about her. If I'm going to be late I think, is she going to starve?

One time I asked this friend to feed her and gave her the key. Then when I got home I couldn't find my key so for half an hour I stood outside trying to get in to feed her. I could hear her crying because she was so upset with me. I thought I can't be doing this to her . . . leaving her for long periods. So now when I do go out, I go out for a short time and then come back. I just decided that I am not going to rely on other people to feed her other than one person—and that person's reliable, but not anyone else. Because I don't feel I can leave her.

How does it feel now when you come home?
If she's inside it's wonderful to come in to see her sitting on the couch happy as a

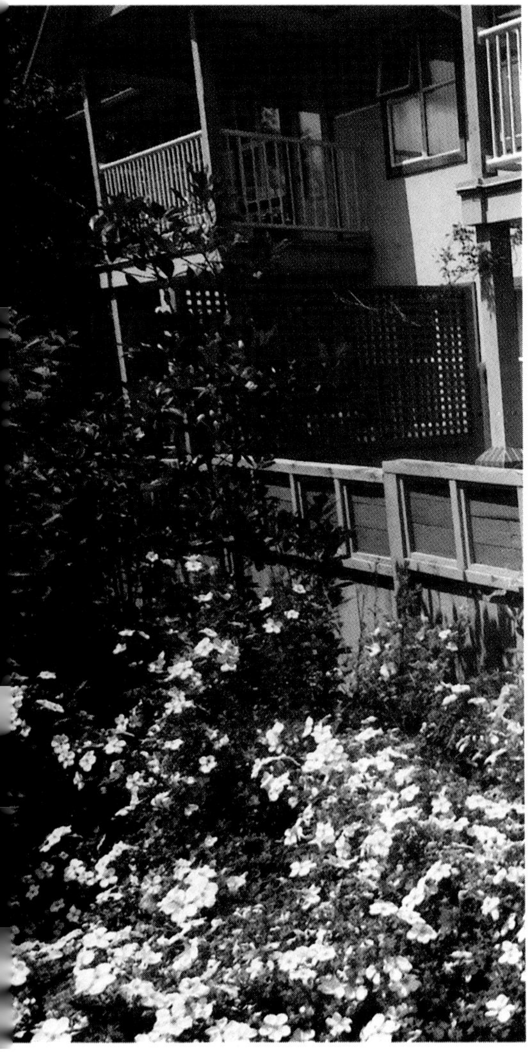

clam. But if she's outside, it's kind of neat. She comes running in like, 'I'm home! You're home!'. Then she wants to come in.

In your writing you talked about loneliness. Has that changed?
It's gone away for the most part. As I say, she's her own kitty. It's been me learning to let her go when she wants. Like we're learning from each other—you do your thing and I'll do mine.

She's asserting her independence too?
I think so. She meows and tells me when she wants to go out. She'll just sit there until I let her out.

Let's talk about your own struggle for independence. It's been a long one for you.
I still don't think I'm totally independent. I think of what people keep telling me: Everybody's interdependent. No one's totally independent.

Why do you feel that you have to be independent?
I guess to me, if I don't be independent I'm a failure. To be able to live on my own . . . being dependent means you have to rely on someone else. If I had a roommate, the roommate and I would have to split half and half who would do what. But with Cuddles I have to do all of it and I really don't mind.

Being independent has always meant a lot to me. When I think of other people who live on their own, they don't have to worry about anyone else but themselves. Now thinking about it, it doesn't make a lot of sense. It makes a lot of sense to be interdependent—with friends around you. But I don't think I would want to be totally dependent on someone else. That's kind of like a failure. If I couldn't look after myself, I would feel like I was relying on someone else. And I've always been taught, don't rely on anyone else but yourself. It's really important as much as possible to do for yourself.

It sounds like having Cuddles has allowed you to maintain that freedom.
Having her is like having a roommate. Like with her, she comes in when she wants, she comes and goes as she wants, and I come and go as I want. It's like a human being, sort of.

Except she doesn't pay the bills.
No, she hasn't learned how to do that.

Was it scary the first time you let her go?
Oh, it was! I just felt, what have I done? Will she ever come back? How will she know where she lives? But she was fine.

Is there anything else?
[Mrrow.]

Oh, that was perfect. We'll end it with a little cry from Cuddles.

BARB'S WRITING

LESS ALONE

When I was in my early twenties I was living at home with Mom and Dad. I wanted to live on my own like my younger brother. I was told by my parents I wasn't ready to live on my own. Mom heard about a group home opening for five women. Mom and Dad and I sat down with a staff of the Association for Mentally Handicapped. I moved in on February 13, 1976. I lived there for a year and a half.

I moved out on my own. I wanted a roommate. I was told no one else was ready to move out. I had support from Mom and Dad and friends at the house. There was no Life Skills workers at the time. When I first moved it was like playing house, doing what I wanted when I wanted. For example, having friends or family over when I wanted. I didn't have to tell anyone when I was going out or when I'd be back. Sometimes it would have been nice to come home to someone to tell about my day and hearing about their day, sharing the bills, cleaning and more.

After 10 years or more a friend asked me if I was interested in having a roommate. I said I might be interested if I knew them. Two weeks went by, then she phoned me at work. She told me she had found me a roommate. The person was sitting in my friend's office. We knew each other. I felt very hurt and angry that they had called me. They were very upset with me because I wouldn't decide at that very moment if the woman could move in or not.

As it turned out, we didn't move in together. My self advocate friend moved into the group home where I had lived.

After I had lived on my own for a while, I thought I would lose my independence

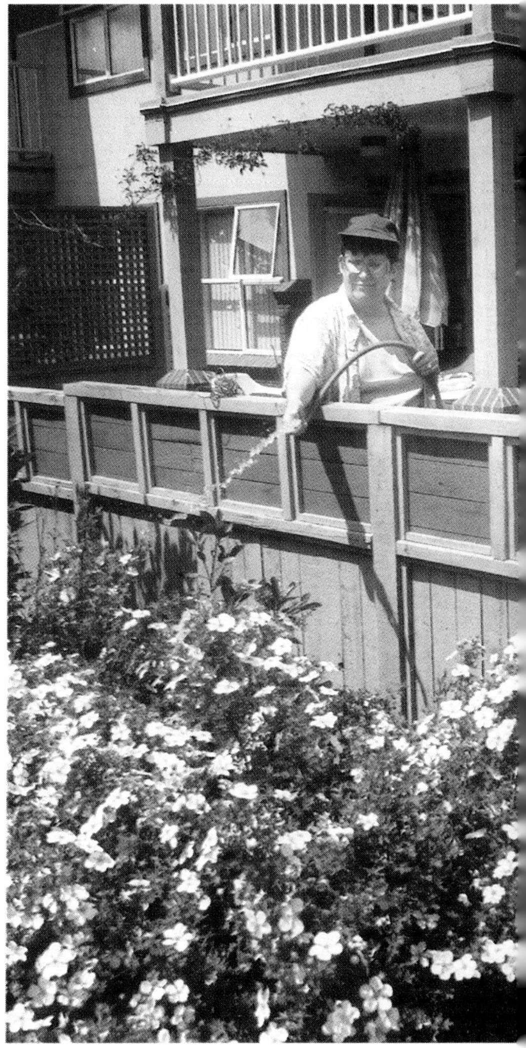

Barb tends a small vegetable plot of her own and also assumes watering duties for the many flowers surrounding the grounds of her co-op.

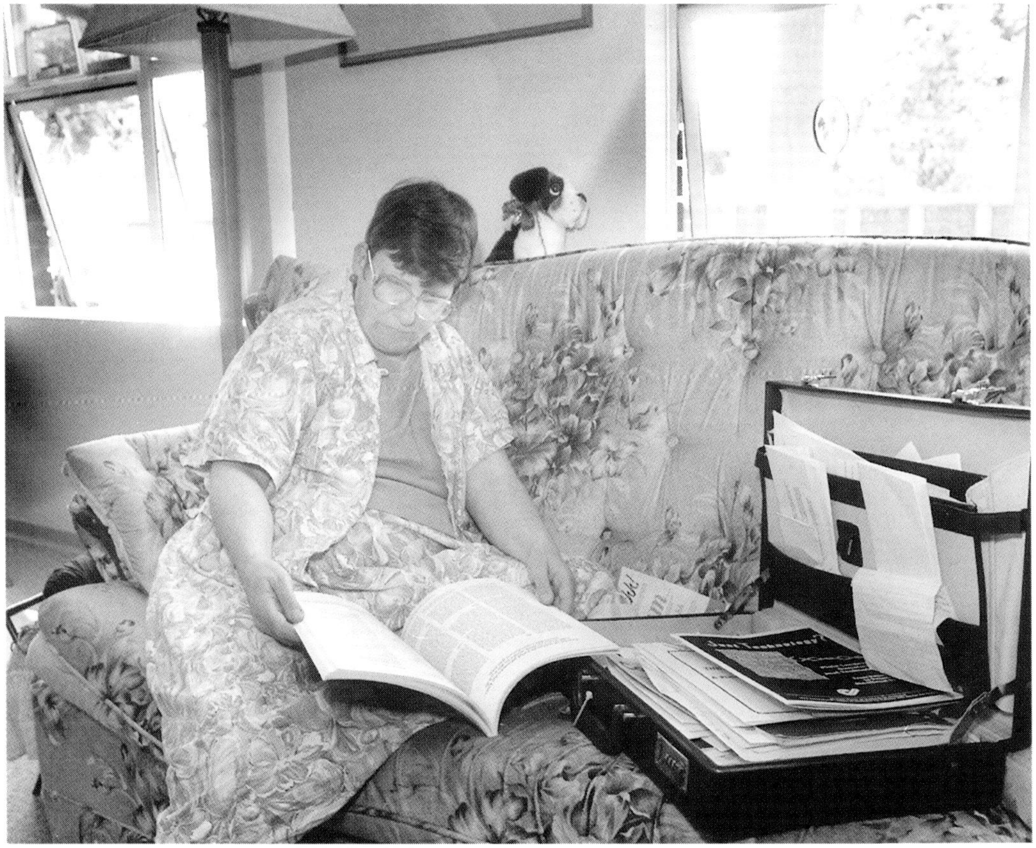

if I got a roommate and that I couldn't do my own business. I thought they wouldn't allow me to do my own banking and paying bills when I was already doing those things on my own.

In the past when I haven't been working that's when it gets tough to pay all my bills. I have managed and whenever problems come up other people think the problem could be solved if I had someone to live with. For example when I don't have a job, people want me to have a roommate to help pay the bills. Now I have been on my own for 18 years. I have often felt alone and wondered how to cope, to try to figure out my own problems. For example, calling a friend or go for a walk. If I got a roommate, I lose my independence and have to support someone else.

I started talking to friends about other solutions. One told me she thought it's neat to have a pet. I told her we're not allowed pets where I live. I thought that it would be

Barb's work in the field of self advocacy takes many forms. Here she checks the transcript of a government health document she rewrote using language more acceptable to people with mental disabilities.

nice. I spoke to the folks where I live about how they would feel if I got a pet. I asked them at a meeting. It was okay with everyone.

One lady who lives upstairs was delighted. She has a pet. She had it before we moved in. Now her pet has company.

The teacher of the daycare told me about a couple at the daycare who were giving away some pets. On May 8th I got CS. She was nine weeks and three days old. I had never had the responsibility of an animal. It felt wonderful and scary at the same time. We both needed each other.

I feel less alone. She is very independent. We hit it off right away. I didn't know much about looking after a cat. A friend who lives upstairs from CS and I, has a boy cat. She has helped us out a lot. I know if I don't know what to do she will know and help out. We have always helped each other out. Now we both have an animal to love and look after.

Preparing for CS's homecoming I had to get food, toys, litter, a box, etc. I made a cosy bed. It was very exciting. Taffy, the cat upstairs, is like a dad to CS.

There are a few people in the apartment building who really didn't want anything to do with me before CS. Now that I have CS there is a woman who wants to see her and hold her.

I don't believe in sterilization (an operation to stop having babies). When it came to thinking about her having babies I didn't feel I could look after CS and her babies. I sat CS down and told her about the operation to not have babies. I felt like a mother talking to her child about their body. I told her I was too young to have grandkittens.

I had to get CS shots to keep her healthy. When I first got CS I kept her on a leash when I took her outside. I showed her the back yard, daycare and other places around home and I carried her around a lot. I still do. I kept her on a leash until she was seven months old. Now she's as free as a bird. I have tried to keep her in when I'm going out. She's happy with that, a very happy cat.

Sometimes she goes to visit Taffy upstairs. One day the lady upstairs phoned me. She asked me if I knew where CS was. I said no I didn't. She said CS was upstairs visiting. Could I send up her pyjamas and toothbrush.

CS is becoming very independent like her Mom. She's great company. She sits at the door when she wants to go out. She stays inside when I go to bed. We have great chats. She loves sitting in an empty bathtub.

I think it's important to tell you that she's very much like her name, Cuddles Snuggles. I have always thought CS is a good name for her.

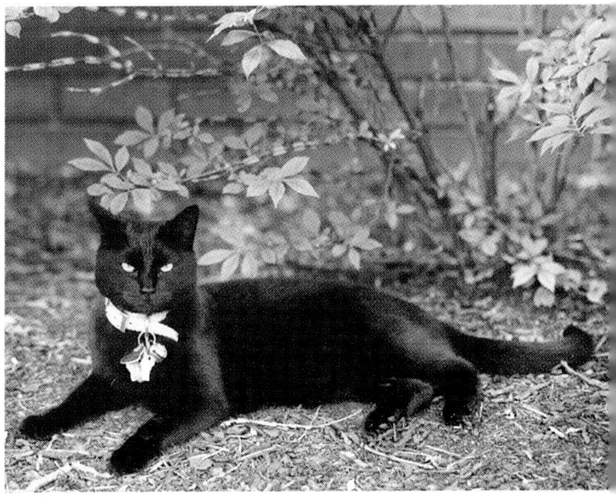

Soon after Barb's interview and writing were completed, CS passed away after being hit by a vehicle.

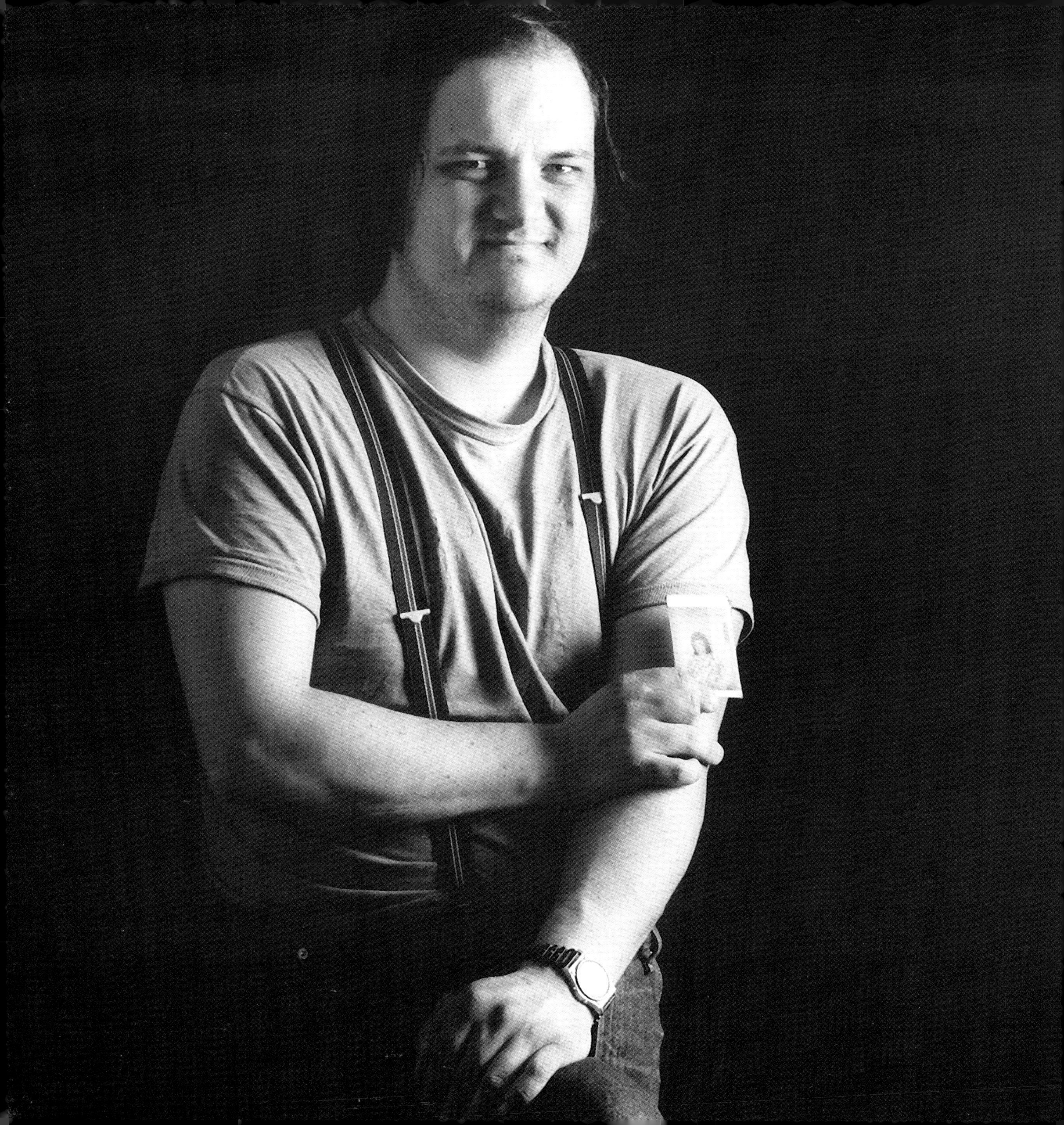

BURT HUNTER

For most of his adult life, Burt (31) has lived with his Dad. He tried living on his own for a while in 1989 but found he couldn't afford the rent. He hopes that one day he will be able to afford to live on his own. Burt is a country music fan. His favourite musicians right now are Alabama and Garth Brooks and he's reading a biography of Anne Murray. Every year Burt hops in his truck and goes to a big country music festival in Merritt. The festival lasts for about four days. Burt has two big dreams. One is to buy a fifth wheel trailer for his truck and spend his time camping; the other is to play guitar and become a country singer.

Burt started going to the Invergarry Learning Centre because he was tired of not being able to read or write very well. Although he got his driver's license by taking an oral test, he wished he could have taken the written one.

Facing page: Burt holds a picture of his mother.

BURT'S STORY

You've said you want to talk about your Mom. What would you like to say about her?
When I was three, I followed two kids across a bridge and I didn't look both ways so I got hit in the process. They ran across and I ran across but I didn't look both ways and I got hit. And what my Mom did is, if it wasn't for my Mom's love . . . who knows where I'd be? Probably in an institution.

You've talked a lot about how important your Mom is to you and how you'd really like to see her. What kind of person is your Mom?
To me she's loving, caring. Right now she's living on Vancouver Island. I would like to go over there one of these days.

What things do you remember about your Mom from when you were a little boy?
The caring. I believe what most people think of is the caring and the love that they gave you.

You got a lot of that from your Mom?
Yes.

How long has it been since you've seen her?
A long time.

More than a year?
Uh huh. But I can't wait to go back over.

What makes it hard for you to visit your Mom?
The money. Mostly the money. The money for the ferry's going up now. Last time I took the ferry it was 35 dollars. But who knows how far it's up now.

What's your best memory of your Mom?
I don't really know.

How does she show you she's caring? What things does she do that let you know that the love and caring are there?
She helps me in some different ways. It's really hard to figure out all the love that she shows. . . .

Do you spend a lot of time with your Dad?
Yes. I'm living with him now.

What is the most important thing for people to know about you?
I would say just caring. Caring and kind. I don't really know after that. It's better to be kind to somebody than cruel. Because if you're cruel they'll walk away from you and not come back to you. And if you're kind, they'll go away and then they'll come back.

Have you had experiences of being cruel to people and they walked away?
I remember in school . . . I was doing something and the teacher wanted me to do it differently, and I told her to "f" off. And after that I went back to my seat and I was thinking about it, and I went right back and I apologized to her. It's better to be kind. To me, if I do something wrong it's going to be with me for a long time. It's better to be loving than a crazy man.

Have you experienced people being cruel to you?
The only thing that I don't like is . . . I don't really like living with my Dad. The only thing I like living with him for is the remembrance of going fishing; and he taught me how to drive a vehicle. He was the only one that taught me an awful lot of things. But some of the times. . . . I believe that you've even had some times that you didn't like being with your parents. I don't like being with my Dad sometimes. He calls me names. It really hurts when you have to listen to it all the time. I don't really like being with my Dad when he goes like that.

It's important to stand up for yourself.
I believe that all these years I never had to stand up for myself. I don't know really how to stand up. So. . . . You have to find out one way or another.

Sounds like it's really hard right now—you have these good memories of your Dad and things he taught you, at the same time you have painful memories.
Sometimes what it feels like is, there are two parts of me, and one part says no, the other part says yes. Some of the times I have to calm myself on what to do. I always go to somebody else—not for information, for peace of mind.

Being able to talk with other people is how you cope with the things that are difficult? Well, that's something most of us do. Is there anything else you want to say? What are the jobs you've had that you remember best?
I was working up in Prince Rupert with my Dad. My Dad's a painter on steel houses, mostly structural steel. He told me about the job. So I quit school and went to work with him. The job was really nice. I painted, sanded rust. I learned how to mix the different paints together, learned how to tie ropes together. I was getting paid five an hour.

I went in with a union. A union job is better because people get paid what they're supposed to get paid, not half what they're supposed to get paid. When you get hurt, the union backs you. If you're not working with the union you don't get backed. When your teeth need work the union backs you. If you have to go to the doctor and things like that, you have to pay a small portion, but the union backs you up on everything.

It was nice working with my Dad. One time he saw me and I wasn't doing anything, and he said if you're not doing anything you're going to get fired. That picked me up right there, and I started moving more.

It was nice up there. We got up at five o'clock, got to the site around six. We sat around having coffee. We'd see the sunrise. It's really nice watching the sunrise when you're sitting down having coffee. At seven o'clock we'd go to work. We'd work till four. After we had to clean up, we headed home.

Your truck seems really important to you. What do you want to say about it?
When I first bought my truck, people told me I couldn't do anything, wasn't worth anything. I believe down deep I thought it was true. Some other people came up to me and said it's not true, to look at myself down deep. I done that and I started realizing that whatever I wanted to do, you have to start with one step at a time and make your goal.

I first got my license in 1984 and I got the truck in 1984. I had an oral exam to get my license. A person tells you the questions and you mark them down. I studied hard

Facing page: Burt says his truck means the world to him: "It gives me my freedom and that is what is important."

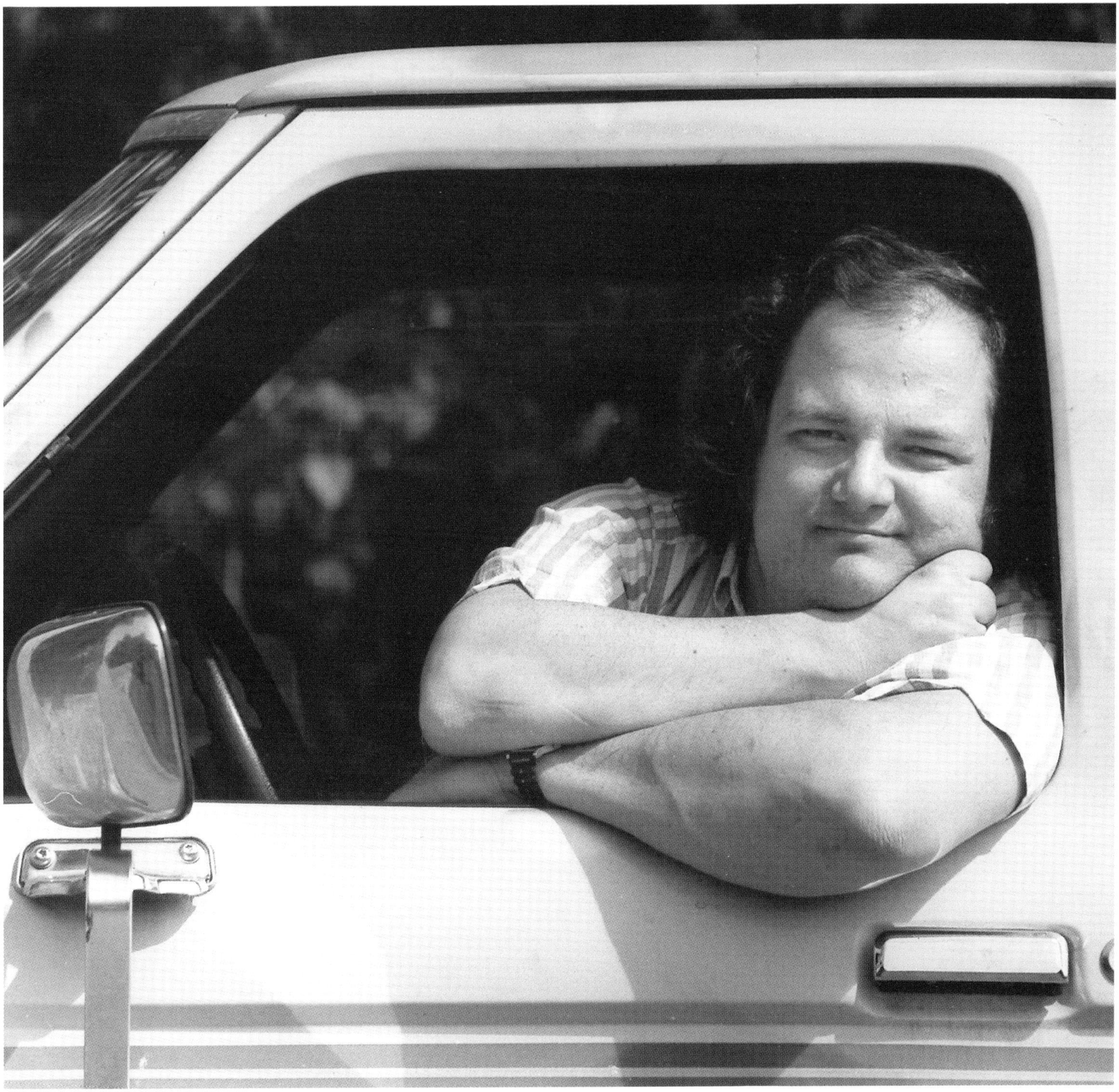

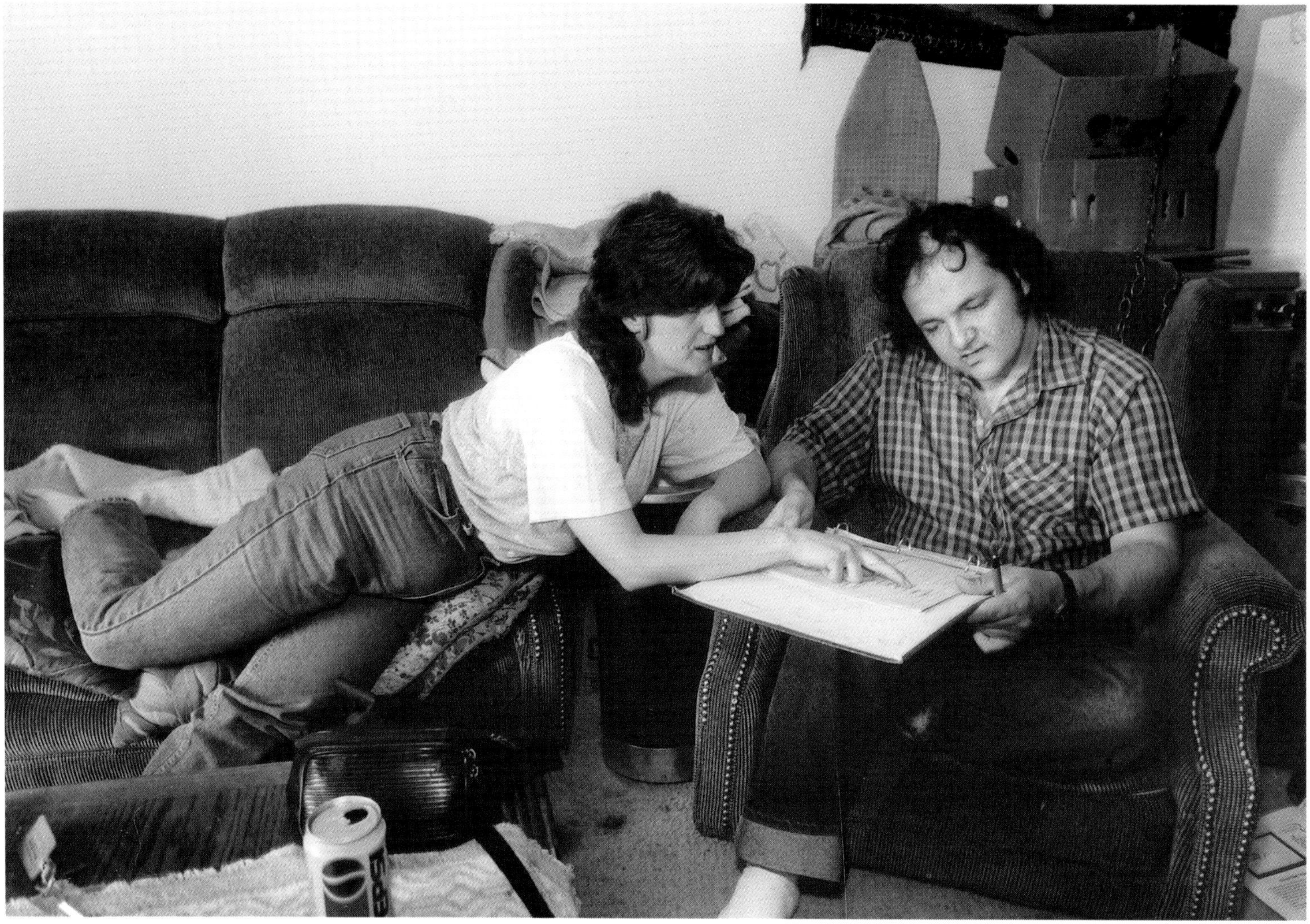

Burt often goes to the apartment of close friend and classmate, Jose Tudor, after school, for relaxation and help with homework. The apartment serves as a second home for Burt during rough times with his father.

for the test. My Dad taught me to drive. He would keep his foot on the gas and brake, and my hands would be on the wheel. He would only take the wheel if I was going off course.

I bought a Ford Ranger. It cost me $13,000. I had the accident when I was three and it was a drinking driver, and I had the money that way. I got the money when I was 19, And I got the truck.

I can go places in the truck, to Vancouver Island and other places. When I first bought the truck, my eyes weren't open; I didn't see life as it is now. I've gone to the

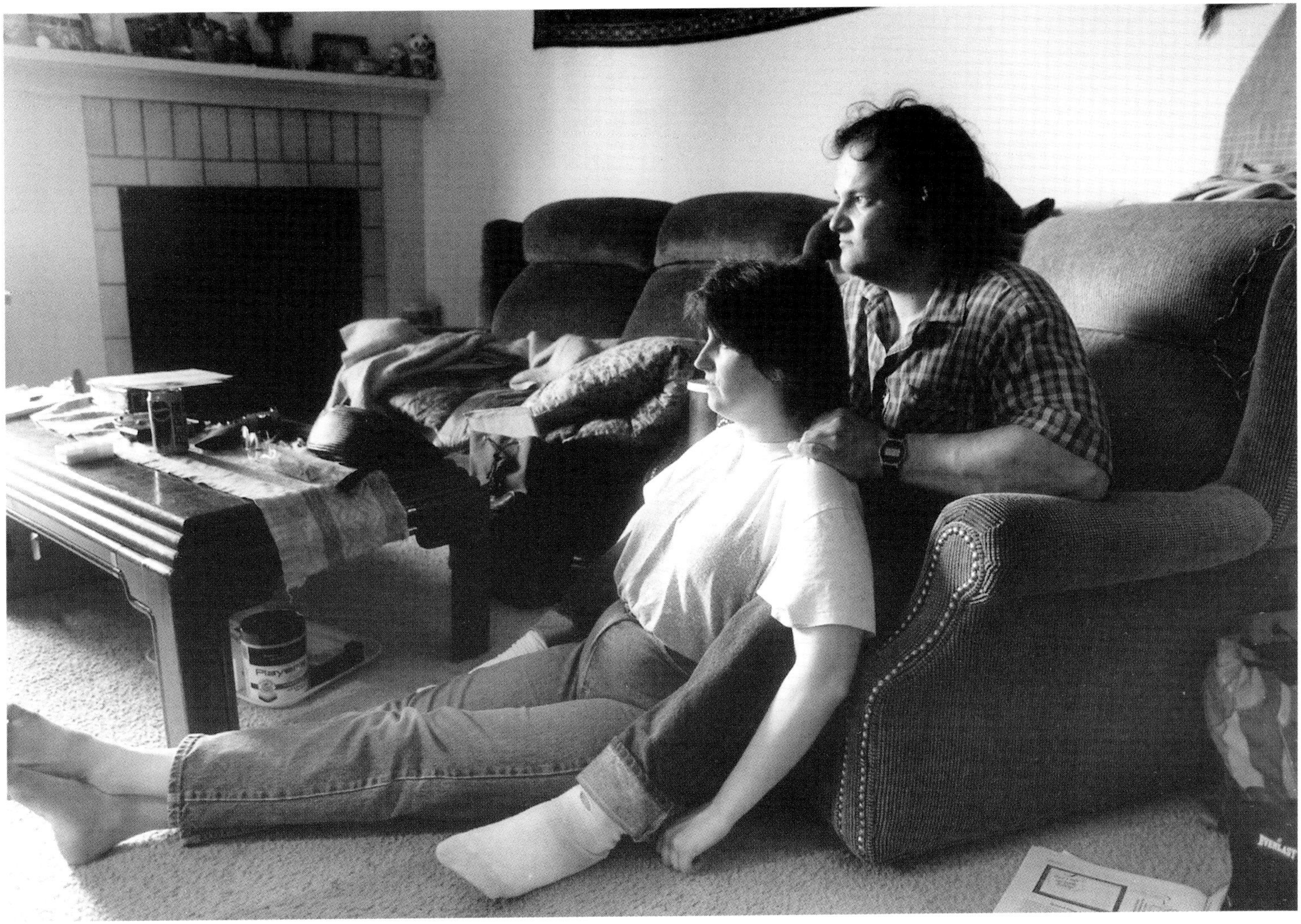

Merritt Music Festival three years in a row now. I have a canopy on the truck and I sleep in it. The ticket was $80 and this year it's $95. My Dad thinks I'm crazy because it's too much money. But it's not his money, or his truck.

You were going to tell us about fly-tying.
I made . . . what is that fly called? A dragon fly? Yes. They have huge bodies and great big wings—four of them. And I made an ant with wings, and used to catch an awful lot on that too. On this lake we caught trout. I believe there was steelhead. And

Accepted as family by Jose and her boyfriend, Burt gives Jose a backrub after studying.

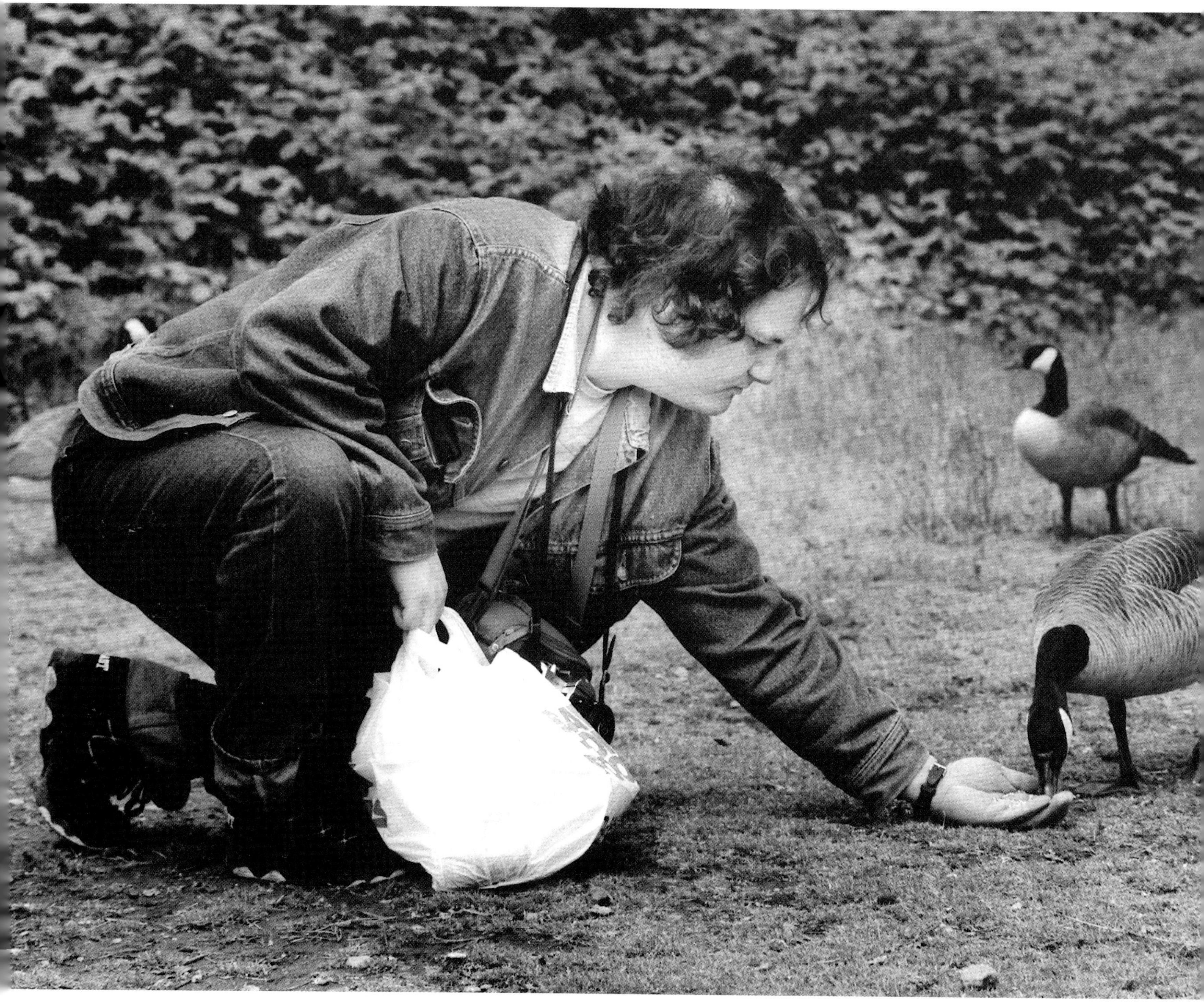

then catfish. It's really nice tying your own flies. It gives you peace of mind, that you can catch your own fish. You need thread, and other stuff, like gauze, hair, anything that makes a hook. Some of the times I went fishing with my Dad and a friend of his. It was really nice going fishing.

Did you have to clean your fish and cook them?
Hah! Most people hated cleaning, but I just adored it. Whenever I caught my fish, took it home, I always cleaned it, scaled it first, then cut the guts out of it.

What was your favorite fish of the ones you caught, and your favorite way to cook it?
The only thing we did was, when we cleaned it, we just put it in batter and after that just throw it on the stove and cooked it. Boy, did it ever taste good.

BURT'S WRITING

FISHING

I believe the first time I went fishing was when I was 18. Because I had an accident when I was three, I don't really know if my memory is all there.

Mostly I went fishing with my Dad and friends of his. The first time I remember fishing for trout and steelhead at a manmade pond.

My Dad had a 14-foot fiberglass boat. We used to go fishing at Stave Lake near Maple Ridge. I remember we used to get stuck in the truck there because there was so much sand around Stave Lake and because there was no road at the time.

When I go fishing with my Dad I never have to think of anything. He was easy with me and didn't push me about fishing—I like it. I discovered fly fishing when we were fishing at Stave Lake. I was watching flies on the water and I saw fish jump out of the water and eat them. I then started to make flies. I got a lot of equipment so I could do fly-tying. My first fly was an ant with wings. I caught a couple of fish with that, then I made other flies. I have about 50 flies now.

Facing page: A class field trip to a local bird sanctuary celebrates Burt's birthday as well. Toting a large bag of bird seed, he coaxes Canada geese to feed. "I love all animals," he says. "They pick up that I'm not going to hurt them."

ABOUT THE EDITORS & PHOTOGRAPHER

JEAN BENNETT: Jean has worked with self advocates and the Association for Community Living movement for many years. She co-wrote the initial project proposal and conducted all the interviews that appear in *So Far*. Jean's sensitivity and uncompromising point of view on behalf of the learners were crucial to the success of this project.

RICHARD JACCOMA: Richard is a novelist, magazine editor, and illustrator. He edited the interviews and writings in *So Far*. Richard's mainstream publishing experience in a variety of disciplines enabled him to make important contributions to the concept, design, creative process, and final outcome of the book.

LEE WEINSTEIN: Lee has worked in literacy for over 20 years, and was the founding administrator of Invergarry Learning Centre. He co-authored the original proposal for *So Far*, served as the project's creative director, in addition to screening participants and leading the writing workshops.

ANN YOW: We were very fortunate to be able to work with the extremely gifted photographer Ann Yow. Ann has photographed for *National Geographic* as well as other magazines and newspapers. She brought an artist's eye to the photo-journalism for *So Far*.